M000020650

Advance Praise for
Convergence Marketing

"The current approaches to communication are no longer enough—the world is saturated with too many messages that overwhelms consumers. Today's marketing communications have to work harder and be more effective than ever before. *Convergence Marketing* guides you through an intuitive approach that turbo-charges your messages, delivering greater impact and leverage of your marketing investment."

—Merle Marting, Senior Vice President,
Global Business, TaylorMade

"Richard Rosen has been a pioneer in bringing the science of direct together with the art of brand. *Convergence Marketing* is a high velocity tour of market tested techniques for combining advertising that moves you with brand direct discipline that compels customers to action."

—Robert L. Solomon, Senior Vice President & Chief
Marketing Officer, Outrigger Enterprises Group

"*Convergence Marketing* is a 'must read' for anyone involved in advanced TV advertising struggling with the disconnect between Media and Creative. As TV advertising becomes more targeted and measurable, it is imperative that these two worlds come together around common objectives. *Convergence Marketing* provides the road map."

—Tony Coulson, Director, Comcast Spotlight

"Rosen combines real world experience with visionary thinking to create an actionable road map to marketing success. Marketers looking to dramatically improve their campaign effectiveness and simultaneously break down organizational silos should read *Convergence Marketing*."

—Ian Oxman, SVP, Marketing Sage Software

"Richard has hit a home run with this book. His ability to break down the language barriers and to build confidence for the C-suite is dynamite. Dynamite that turns into profits. In today's cluttered and noisy market empathizing with the customer and building a nurturing relationship is what it is all about. Richard Rosen gets it. And you will too by using the principles as laid out in this book."

—Thomas M Shannon, Director, Revenue Management (retired),
Puget Sound Energy

"*Convergence Marketing* is the manual all marketers have been waiting for! Richard Rosen has distilled in a very handy book, the lessons of a life-time as a practitioner of marketing and advertising. This is a handbook designed to give real help, real advice and real results! It is easy to read, well documented with case studies and examples, and full of wisdom. Whether you are a CEO, CFO, CIO, or in marketing, sales or advertising, whenever you are looking at brand building, or planning marketing strategies, advertising or sales, read this book. It has something in it for you."

—Alastair Tempest, Director General, Federation of
European Direct & Interactive Marketing (FEDMA)

"Very relevant for today's advertising and marketing executives who struggle with finding solutions that meet both brand and sales objectives. Rosen's Velocity Scale™ is an effective analytical tool to improve your investment and creative decision-making skills. Valuable to anyone interested in making brand advertising far more accountable."

—Becky Chidester, President,
Wunderman, New York

"What we have here is a 'failure to communicate' because many of the fundamental assumptions we make about how people consume media need to be challenged and rethought. That's just what Richard Rosen does in this book—and he goes even further by outlining pathways to focus and converge media streams to create business impact in today's world. A great and practical read for anyone in business communications."

—Ralph A. Oliva, Executive Director, Institute for the Study of
Business Markets, Penn State

"*Convergence Marketing* is a solution whose time has come. In a world where the economic pressures are driving the need for more effective growth, Richard has come up with a simple and compelling roadmap that brings together the best of advertising and the best of business. This is one of those books that you are going see on a lot of successful executive's desks. Don't miss it."

—Pam Maphis Larrick, Former CEO of FCBi Worldwide and
CEO of MRM Partners Worldwide

"The Rosen Velocity Scale™ is a powerful and relevant tool for 21st century marketers. Rosen's message ought not to be ignored. He is urging marketers to innovate and march forward by building on his successes. What better time than NOW to rewrite the rules of marketing."

—Ann M. Jelito, President, Right Time Coaching and Consulting,
Formerly Sr. Director of Training, Association of National
Advertisers (ANA)

"As a leader of major service businesses, I know that marketing is important—but all of that brand, image, direct, indirect—it can make an operations executive's head spin. Using the Rosen Velocity Scale™ can help me target my message to my customer and make an investment that yields real returns using scarce resources to benefit my business."

—Chris Wallace, Senior Vice President,
Customer Services, NCR Corporation

"Business schools and marketing books teach countless lessons from the likes of Microsoft, Intel, Nike, and Starbucks. Yet few of us work in multi-billion-dollar companies with gross margins north of 60 percent, that is, with a lot of marketing slack in the system. For the rest of us, Richard Rosen has helpful advice. Namely, get your brand building and direct marketing to converge for more acceleration in the customer's buying process. This is a pragmatic book for the marketing veteran and novice alike."

—Kevin Renner, Global Marketing Director, FEI Company

"*Convergence Marketing* provides a practical and innovative guide for all levels of management to balance brand-building tools with powerful direct marketing techniques. Rosen draws on a wealth of personal experience and dozens of real examples to explain why convergence between brand building and DM matters and exactly how it can be achieved faster driving more profits. This is a must read for anyone who wants to get the most out of their efforts to communicate effectively and efficiently with customers."

—Dennis R. Howard, Dean and Philip H. Knight Professor of Business
Charles H. Lundquist College of Business, University of Oregon

"This is a book that the business world has been waiting many years for. My company has been a keen follower of Richard Rosen's theories for many years and his methods have brought us great successes across a number of products and brands, so I would strongly recommend this book to anyone who wishes to significantly improve their marketing and advertising ROI. *Convergence Marketing* is sure to become the industry bible for bridging the gap between brand building and direct response. It will give you all the necessary tools to efficiently leverage your every marketing dollar; to not only alert customers of your presence, but to lead them to actively respond, build relationships with you, and most importantly buy from you."

—Sandi Cesko, President Studio Moderna—Ljubljana, Slovenia

"*Convergence Marketing* underscores the fact that most marketing is going direct. The combination of brand and direct highlights the power of direct, encompassing relevance and responsibility, leading to results."

—John A. Greco Jr., President & CEO,
Direct Marketing Association

"Marketing professionals are now living in a world of 'and'. Push-and-pull communications; offline and online; print and video; paid and non-paid media. Effectiveness demands leveraging this and it demands integrating marketing communications around and for the consumer. *Convergence Marketing* does a great job of illustrating why and how."

> —Tom Collinger, Associate Dean and Department Chair,
> Medill Integrated Marketing Communications
> Program, Northwestern University

"Richard Rosen's book shows you how to maximize the benefits of brand advertising—and the best of direct—it does not create a false merger but combines the best of both disciplines. It is based on a thorough understanding of the customer and their point in sales cycle. The final touch, which really matters, is how by using appropriate financial measures a company can measure the value of its customer profitability.

I thoroughly recommend this book. It is full of antidotal business examples which bring practicality to the text. The tools and processes covered, if followed properly, will deliver accountability, scalability, and consistency."

> —Professor Derek Holder, FIDM, Managing Director and Founder,
> The Institute of Direct Marketing

"I have been looking for something like Rosen's Velocity Scale™ for years. This will let me talk with my clients using a language we can all understand. And the fact that I can provide immediate response at each level of the scale will help me guide my clients in spending their shrinking marketing dollars wisely. Richard Rosen makes this concept clear and simple. I can't wait to begin using it."

> —Betsy Ashton, Marketing and Public Relations Consultant,
> BearingPoint

"*Convergence Marketing: Combining Brand and Direct for Unprecedented Profits* is perhaps the most important and thoughtful book on how to sell to customers at a distance since Lester Wunderman's *Being Direct*. It is my sincere wish that this book be translated into as many languages as possible to enable marketers worldwide to benefit from the wisdom and sheer practical beauty of this book. It will bring together the finance, sales, marketing and direct marketing functions and enable them to understand this kind of marketing exercise from each of their respective professional needs viewpoints. This deserves to be considered by every marketer to be a must-read, and she should buy extra copies for finance and sales."

> —Charles Prescott, Vice President,
> International Direct Marketing Association, USA

CONVERGENCE
MARKETING

CONVERGENCE MARKETING

Combining Brand and Direct for Unprecedented Profits

RICHARD G. ROSEN

WITH JANE ROSEN

Nov, 2015

Brett,

Here is to empathy and accountability while having fun along our road,

all my best,

Richard

WILEY

JOHN WILEY & SONS, INC.

Copyright © 2009 by Richard Rosen. All rights reserved.

Published by John Wiley & Sons, Inc., Hoboken, New Jersey.
Published simultaneously in Canada.

No part of this publication may be reproduced, stored in a retrieval system, or transmitted in any form or by any means, electronic, mechanical, photocopying, recording, scanning, or otherwise, except as permitted under Section 107 or 108 of the 1976 United States Copyright Act, without either the prior written permission of the Publisher, or authorization through payment of the appropriate per-copy fee to the Copyright Clearance Center, Inc., 222 Rosewood Drive, Danvers, MA 01923, (978) 750-8400, fax (978) 646-8600, or on the Web at www.copyright.com. Requests to the Publisher for permission should be addressed to the Permissions Department, John Wiley & Sons, Inc., 111 River Street, Hoboken, NJ 07030, (201) 748-6011, fax (201) 748-6008, or online at http://www.wiley.com/go/permissions.

Limit of Liability/Disclaimer of Warranty: While the publisher and author have used their best efforts in preparing this book, they make no representations or warranties with respect to the accuracy or completeness of the contents of this book and specifically disclaim any implied warranties of merchantability or fitness for a particular purpose. No warranty may be created or extended by sales representatives or written sales materials. The advice and strategies contained herein may not be suitable for your situation. You should consult with a professional where appropriate. Neither the publisher nor author shall be liable for any loss of profit or any other commercial damages, including but not limited to special, incidental, consequential, or other damages.

For general information on our other products and services please contact our Customer Care Department within the United States at (800) 762-2974, outside the United States at (317) 572-3993 or fax (317) 572-4002.

Wiley also publishes its books in a variety of electronic formats. Some content that appears in print may not be available in electronic books. For more information about Wiley products, visit our Web site at www.wiley.com.

Library of Congress Cataloging-in-Publication Data
Rosen, Richard G.
  Convergence marketing : combining brand and direct for unprecedented profits / Richard G. Rosen with Jane Rosen.
      p.   cm.
    Includes index.
    ISBN 978-0-470-16493-8 (cloth)
      1. Branding (Marketing)   2. Direct marketing.   3. Marketing.   I. Rosen, Jane.
II. Title.
  HF5415.1255.R67 2009
  658.8—dc22

                                                                          2008042914

Printed in the United States of America.

10 9 8 7 6 5 4 3 2 1

To Jane—my wife,
best friend, and partner.

Contents

CONTENTS

PART III

INTRODUCTION

Two roads diverged in a wood and I—
I took the one less traveled by,
and that has made all the difference.

—ROBERT FROST

After 20 years toiling in the trenches of the advertising industry, this book grew out of my quest to converge two disciplines of thought. My first job out of business school led me down the road of direct marketing. Soon after, another road led me to advertising. I realized that each school was steeped in brilliance, yet lacking in so many ways. I wanted to bring those separate roads together and create a new path that would gain better traction. It was suddenly so clear that if we could utilize the disciplines of both direct and brand advertising, while respecting the needs of the customer, we'd have a better set of tools and processes to deliver what the C-suite needs—accountability, scalability, projectability, and consistency—faster and with less money.

So here's the result—your primer on how to successfully bring the school of advertising and the school of business together! Because convergence grew out of my frustration with the gap between those two worlds, I know I'm not the only one feeling it. I have experienced similar frustrations with clients and peers. This is the logical direction in which our industry has been moving for years. We've all sat in too many meetings watching adversaries from the brand and direct departments speaking to each other in foreign languages without an interpreter in the room. What a waste. Why not participate in an empathetic dialogue with our colleagues? We need a common language and tools that will help us work together toward our shared goal: to make money and build brand resonance. That's why a palatable new vocabulary is part of the critical path for ease of acceptance. You'll learn new words and terms like *brand-interaction* as you are introduced to the convergence toolbox.

The other essential element to make convergence work is a visual common ground. During my years of dialogue with both brand and direct practitioners, I have developed a process tool called the Rosen Velocity Scale. One of my clients, a VP of branding, calls it the killer application. It's a tool that brings visual understanding of the balance between brand and direct. It's used to determine the goals of the communication, so everyone involved can see them—and then deliver!

Finally, we must get the sales and finance functions on board. As the adoption curves of customer relationship management (CRM) have shown, we can progress much faster if the executive suite embraces this change—especially if it embraces the model of real-time accountability. We have the technology; it's time to use it! For the same reason billions are streaming into the web as the next frontier, convergence marketing is the new toolbox to deliver accountability and profits with reduced business risk from both offline and online media.

Unlike the earlier attempts of integration marketing, convergence brings the disciplines of brand and direct together like never before—to generate profits your budget never dreamed of. It is the culmination of our past successes into newly refined processes and creative tools that build brand resonance through interaction. So let's get started!

What I'm offering is a new set of glasses. Put them on, and see what a difference this new perspective called convergence makes as you join me on this new road that most could not see until now.

—RICHARD ROSEN

CONVERGENCE
MARKETING

I

Convergence of Brand and Direct

1

WHY CONVERGENCE
MARKETING?

We live in a world that revolves around the individual. We celebrate self-expression at every turn, within the personalization of every product we buy. We pursue personal desires; we constantly download music, games, and films on communication devices that fit into our back pockets. And the individual controls it all. This is a far cry from the way we've always done it. These days, individuals decide not only *how* marketers and advertisers can reach them, but also *if and when* we can reach them at all. If they are inclined to grant us access, they choose *where and how* the communication takes place. The individual controls his or her relationship with the brand. The only way those of us in marketing and advertising can regain some leverage is to love the individual. We need to empathize with him or her, respect him or her. We need to gain the individual's trust so he or she will trust the brand, which gives us what both sides want—enduring brand loyalty. The best way to achieve this is by combining the best tools from the two major marketing disciplines, brand building and direct marketing.

Convergence is the happy union of the best of brand and direct. It also includes tools from sales. All of these tools are fused to build loyalty, through a respectful and empathetic dialogue with the freethinking, experiential individual known as our customer. Convergence retains the powerful imagery and messaging of brand advertising, while leveraging the motivational techniques of direct marketing, and focusing all of it on the goals set by sales. It is powered by a financial model that statistically determines the expected worth of the individual, and it all happens in real time. This all adds up to making money faster than ever before, and it has the unique advantage of being a process we can repeat over and over again, as well as proving critical path accountability to the corporate financial officer (CFO).

The theory of convergence has evolved out of my own experience within the school of business and the school of advertising. After all, I am a card-carrying, MBA-trained, business-minded guy, who loves creative advertising. So this methodology strives to bring together the left and right brains for the most effective possible work. It unites creative and financial, strategic and intuitive, in a collaborative effort to reach a shared goal. That goal just so happens to be our primary job requirement: to make money. It's about building brand, increasing sales, and improving the bottom line.

Although convergence is a new model, as a practitioner you're already halfway there because it's about using what you already know from your discipline and combining it with the other half you haven't really met. It's a proven model, with pragmatic tools to guide us into the next phase of our craft. Convergence marketing is the logical next leap for advertisers and marketers looking to deliver greater results and profits in today's increasingly competitive global economy.

The benefits are tremendous and measurable. Using the new tools, we can balance and leverage resources to drive brand and demand via all media and channels. At the same time, we'll create an environment where everyone can work together, bringing his or her best to colleagues at the table, rather than competing against each other in the same tired silos.

EARLY CROSSROADS: WHEN TWO PATHS CONVERGED

I've been developing this method for over 30 years—a journey that began when I was a franchise marketing manager for Kawasaki Motors Corporation's northeast region. It was my second job out of college as an undergraduate, and I was raring to go. It was my dream job. As a teenager I loved motorcycles, and rebuilt my first bike at age 16. I got a job working on bikes after school at a local shop, and I loved everything about them. I even spent weekends road racing bikes, at speeds cresting 125 mph and now the "man" was paying me to ride.

I left the evergreen-filled campus of the University of Oregon for the not-so-green turnpikes of Highland Park, New Jersey. I lived right at the crossroads of Route Nine, Route One, the

New Jersey Turnpike, and the Garden State Parkway. Newark Airport was up the road, just past the three refineries. I can still see the sunrise through the smokestacks over the Jersey shore.

At Kawasaki, my job was to market the concept of fun with fast motors attached.

The tag line for Kawasaki was right on: "We Know Why You Ride." It was strong, macho, and speed-oriented. They were speaking to me, their target audience, a bike lover through and through. Their agency, J. Walter Thompson, was right on the money. But I knew there had to be more we could do to sell these great bikes. After all, I was young, passionate, highly competitive, and ready to sell franchises.

All of the dealers relied on mass advertising, mostly print ads, to build brand and drive traffic. Kawasaki advertised in all the trade magazines, as well as any others that targeted men aged 16 to 24. But I wanted them to draw bike lovers like me into the shop. I mean, if you sent me an invitation to come by and test drive one of those babies, you'd have had me by the chaps, if you know what I mean! So why weren't we doing that? It seemed easy enough. They were spending somewhere in the area of $5,000,000 on print advertising, a few TV spots, tradeshows, and bike races. That was a lot of money back then; yet we were only reaching a small percentage of our target. All of this money was going into print ads that were creative, on message and gorgeous, but didn't get guys into the shop. Our director of advertising knew he didn't have enough money to drive the frequency he needed to accomplish his task.

I, of course, wanted sales to move faster. I just knew if we sent out an invitation to guys like me to come in and take a test drive, we'd be in business. These were great bikes, and after all, this is where the rubber hit the road! What a great compliment it would be to the strategy of building brand awareness. Then I discovered that we had access to about eighty percent of all the Department of Motor Vehicles (DMV) records across the United States, and we could get a biker's address just by asking. Man, oh, man, this was perfect; it just made sense. But when I suggested it to the higher-ups, I was told to stick to doing the franchise marketing I was hired to do. So I did . . . for the time being.

That experience has always stayed with me. It was the catalyst for all of my investigations into marketing and sales. I guess you could say it was the moment of inspiration for this methodology because I suddenly understood both the buyer and the seller. I knew how to make both happy, and it just didn't make sense to disregard an idea like the invitation to the store. Using the language I know now, I guess my question was, why not enhance the brand message with a call to action to get the individual to move forward in the sales process? Why not give our target the brand experience *on the road*, by converging the paths of brand and direct? And I wasn't even the big stakeholder—just a kid who wanted to sell franchises where these great bikes flew off the shelves at record-breaking speed. Why not combine great creative and a decisive call to action?

The Traditional Model versus Building Brand and Demand

The simple logic of combining certain elements of brand and direct was crystal clear to this rebellious kid. Kawasaki and the agency were doing a great job, using what they knew best.

My idea didn't have any traction, but I didn't know why. It wasn't until a few years later that I realized just how much I didn't know about the cultural and political dynamics that made it impossible for my idea to work—not just at Kawasaki, but in almost every company. In fact, it wasn't until I completed my MBA that I could see the problem.

The traditional model of advertising is a relic of the 1960s, when advertising was in its heyday and Madison Avenue ruled. The best way to describe the essence of that model is, "If we build it, they will come." It still works in a few cases, like the partnership of Nike and Wieden + Kennedy. Of course, they have hundreds of millions of dollars to spend on building awareness. It costs a lot to rise above the clutter these days. And they have the visionary chief executive officer (CEO) who supports the "spend." And you know what? We do come. The same holds for Apple. They spend a lot of money on awareness, and they have Steve Jobs, the brilliant, driven entrepreneur, to enforce the spend. Both also have the key ingredient of brilliant creative. Do they know how to appeal to their targets or what?

The traditional model works at their level because they have three necessary variables: (1) millions to spend, (2) the consistent, visionary, and driven CEO, and (3) the kicker—a product that is at parity or better. So look at Phil Knight at Nike, Steve Jobs at Apple, Richard Branson at Virgin, (and Andy Grove at Intel, to name a few). Each is a consistent CEO, the visionary who was also the driver of the brand and approves spending an outrageous amount of money necessary to get past today's clutter. Their products are at parity or better. And it works. How many of us have these three things?

What happens when you *don't* have these three essential elements and try to emulate the model? Witness Steve Case, the former CEO of AOL. Where was his vision? Was his product just okay rather than at parity? AOL needed him to lead the charge in the Time Warner-AOL merger and, well, you know the story.

THE TRADITIONAL MODEL OF CLASSIC ADVERTISING

The traditional model I'm referring to stems from the Attention, Interest, Desire, and Action (AIDA) model of the 1960s. However, I've updated the terms to better fit our current experience and make it easier to comprehend. According to this model, if we build 100 percent Awareness *(Attention)* for the product, then 80 percent will have Preference *(Interest)* for my product, 60 percent will Consider *(Desire)* it, 40 percent will Buy it *(Action)*. So here's the model from which most of us came. This is the school of advertising as we know it, and this is the model most advertising people still use. But does it work for you? If I gave you enough money to create 100 percent awareness of your product, would you end up with 40 percent sales? If you think you would, please call me because I'd love to see your work. Please see Figure 1.1 to review this classic traditional model we all grew up with.

As I've traveled the world for the past 20 years, I've posed this question over and over to audiences at corporations and professional marketing conferences: "Does the current model work for you?" Few, if any, people raise their hands. So, as a good marketer, I ask another targeted question, "Do any of you believe this model works?" And around the world, people from

Figure 1.1   Traditional Model

Traditional Advertising Model

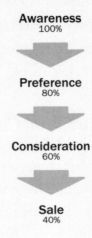

Awareness
100%

Preference
80%

Consideration
60%

Sale
40%

all levels of management admit that it hasn't worked for years. So *why are we still using it?*

THE BUSINESS REASON FOR CHANGE

On average, no more than 5 percent to 10 percent of all companies have the three variables necessary to make the model work: the visionary CEO, a large advertising budget to afford repetition, and a product at parity or better. These companies also have big agencies creating beautiful, award-winning campaigns. It stands to reason that other agencies would try to emulate these big fish. Unfortunately, these smaller agencies have clients who want the cool creative element but lack those three strategic variables. They're just not in the same league. That leaves 90 percent of businesses out there searching for the next big thing, spending tons of money on media, trying to substantiate every-thing they have produced—yet they can't possibly be successful with this antiquated model. It's a set up for disaster, and no one wins. Worse, the CFO cuts the advertising and marketing budget because it looks like a huge waste of money. It reminds me of getting my allowance cut back the first time I spent it all on candy. It was only later that I learned to make better choices in managing my funds!

Age of Accountability

It's now imperative that we be accountable for our spending. It never used to be so tough, but we have entered the Age of Accountability. It's "post-Enron" behavior. Ever since the Sarbanes-Oxley Act of 2002, your CFO is demanding accounta-bility throughout the organization, and that includes every dol-lar spent on advertising and marketing—and it's a pain. The good news is, if you use this new methodology and the financial tools in the upcoming chapters, you could be the rock star who turns your marketing and advertising departments into a profit center rather than a line-item expense.

The False Promise of Integration

Remember *integration*? It was one of the highlights of the 1980s, right up there with disco and Bananarama. Integration was the catch-all strategy of the day—except that it meant something different for everyone. The reason I bring this up is to clarify, right here and now, that convergence is *not* integration. Granted, it seemed like a good idea to those of us who were in marketing and advertising back then. But so did shoulder pads and big hair. Integration was supposed to create an environment where all disciplines of brand, direct, sales, and public relations (PR) worked in harmony. It did help us understand the possibility of this happening in the future, but it was a huge disruption for the established culture of silos. Everyone knew his or her place, with marketing over here, advertising over there, sales down the hall, and direct in the basement. Like in *West Side Story*, the Jets and the Sharks did not mingle. And here comes integration trying to get the kids to play nice. Gee, Officer Krupke, Krup you![1]

Just when integration became the fad, I became managing director of a new division, PSW Direct, at Pihas Schmidt Westerdahl, a medium-sized general advertising and public relations agency in Portland, Oregon. They hired me to create a direct marketing unit to round out their portfolio. (Apparently they had gotten the memo on integration.) My first clue that direct was not held in high esteem was the location of my office. It was on the lowest floor of the firm and filled with used furniture. I felt like Rodney Dangerfield—I got no respect! This was confirmed the day I placed my integrated campaign, which had earned millions for U.S. Bank, onto the desk of the creative director. He took one look, shoved it aside, and yelled in my general direction, "Get this crap off my desk." Ah, happy times.

Several years into this experiment, the concept hadn't even left the starting gate. There we were, 60 of us from six divisions,

---

[1] Stephen Sondheim (lyrics), and Leonard Bernstein (music), "Gee, Officer Krupke," *West Side Story*.
West Side Story © 1961 United Artists Pictures, Inc. All Rights Reserved.

pretending to work in harmony. Everyone remained safe in his or her silo, and integration was nothing more than a concept. Nothing tied us together, and our different business philosophies made it impossible to even start a conversation.

Bored with the entire set up, I decided to grow my division. We combined brand and direct marketing tools with real-time measurability and the use of all media. The division grew like it was on steroids. We picked up huge portions of U.S. Bank, Disney, First Interstate Bank, Pacific Power, Puget Power, Washington Water Power, Florida Power and Light, Sybase, Dell, IBM, Intel, Novell, and Sequent. We made more money with 10 people than the entire general agency did with 40. We were unstoppable. We had real-time measurability and effective behavioral change agents within the communication. It was working. Everything we did turned to gold. I'd been a catalyst for change for all of our clients, who were getting amazing results. Our largest client, Pacific Power, had over 700,000 customers in seven western states. We were a marketing machine, creating and launching new products faster than anyone had ever seen in that space. It was the kick in the pants I needed to start my own agency.

Brand Resonance

Now we're all in search of brand resonance. I'm all for it, but because the old model doesn't cut it for 90 percent of us, how do we do it? How can we build meaningful brands with respect to the individual?

In *A New Brand World: 8 Principles for Achieving Brand Leadership in the Twenty-First Century*, Scott Bedbury and Stephen

Fenichell define what a brand is and what it is not. We need to change our perspective in regard to our relationship with the brand in order to expand brand relevance and brand resonance. Bedbury and Fenichell suggest, "Perhaps this is the greatest single change in the concept of 'brand' in recent years. Where we once looked at brands on a surface level, we now view them in more intimate and multi-dimensional terms. We plumb their depths, looking for reassurance that they are good, responsible, sensitive, knowing, and hip."[2]

As smart marketers, we need a new way of thinking that uses every means available to touch the individual with the brand. It must encompass every aspect of the relationship, from the way we build interaction on the web site to the way we answer the phone. We have to create a meaningful and positive experience at every turn.

The End of the Traditional Model: A Fond Farewell

Our world has changed, so we have to change how we deliver strategically driven creative. Most of us are forced to live within a box that someone else has arbitrarily drawn, along with a budget that is designated to a specific line item, which bears no relation to what needs to get done. So let's change the rules. Let's mix it up a little bit—okay, let's mix it up a lot! After all, this is what the CXOs are demanding—a new way of thinking, which does *not* consist of "just add web!"

---

[2]Scott Bedbury and Stephen Fenichell, *A New Brand World: 8 Principles for Achieving Brand Leadership in the Twenty-First Century* (New York: Viking, 2002), 3.

Building Brand and Demand: Changing the Model

One of the most important variables in convergence marketing is the power of measurement and finance "in real time." It drives success. Using the best of brand and direct, we can build brand and demand simultaneously, through interaction. The sooner we begin the one-on-one dialogue, the faster we can build the relationship between our brand and individuals. But the key is in earning their trust, and we have to start from square one. After all, they may not know anything about us, or they might not even like us. We need to find out where their heads are so we can get the right message to them. Otherwise, we could botch the entire relationship. The only way to achieve this is by starting with empathy. We all need to care about the brand, and I mean every aspect of the brand. It is what the company stands for, the tone, pride of product, and all of those wonderful attributes that truly make for a brilliant brand. We also need to care about what it's worth in real time, not because its fun to run numbers, but because we can leverage what we've accomplished and replicate it with precision via all media. Rather than recreating the wheel each time, we can replicate our success and make bigger money, faster. It's what we've been hired to do, and we should all want it to go faster.

Vive la Différence!

The new model differs from the old by quickly getting the individual to interact with the brand, via one-on-one dialogue, via all media. Looking at Figure 1.2, we can compare the steps of the new model to the old. In the new model, we move from awareness to engagement to interaction. This means that the ad must

Figure 1.2 Traditional Model versus Convergence

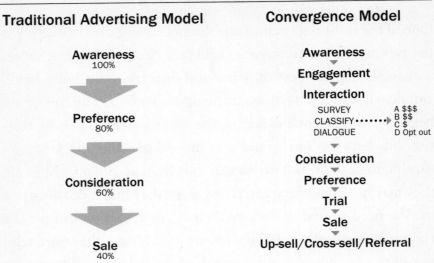

work much harder from the beginning so that individuals will raise their hands. Once they raise their hands, we can ask them a few questions, borrowing from Sales 101. Based upon those questions, we are able to classify them into A, B, C, or D leads. And, once we know their level of interest, we know *how* to talk to them, with empathy so that we can begin a meaningful, trusting relationship. We won't waste their time or push them too far; we will listen with empathy and treat them with respect.

It is this respectful behavior that will move them toward consideration and preference, trial and sale. And, from there, we simply guide them to the next level.

This is the basic layout of the model, and we'll go through each step in detail. But, before we get there, we need learn how to talk to each other—from branding to direct, to sales, to information technology (IT), and all the way to the executive suite. We need a common language supported by our shared goal.

2

GETTING TO CONVERGENCE
With the Common Language of Respect

Today, it's all about reaching the individual. And frankly, the only way to reach out to individuals and not get your hand smacked is to understand the power of empathy when building your relationships with them.

But before we can begin our empathetic dialogue with the customer, we must figure out how to talk to our pals just down the hall. That's right, we have to work together; brand, direct, and even the folks in sales. To pull this off, we need a common language that helps us understand what each brings to the table and how we can best use our combined knowledge to achieve our goal. After all, if our goal is to earn the trust of the individual through empathetic dialogue, we need to practice what we preach right here at home. The key word is *empathy*. Through empathy, we gain respect for each other, for ourselves, and for the individual—a trifecta of mutual respect.

So let's not argue about semantics. We can all work together toward the same goal if we base our language around the need for empathizing with the individual. Empathy, simply put, is about identifying with and understanding someone's situation and feelings. If we understand individuals' hearts and minds, their needs and desires, we can build trust by touching them in ways that matter most. It all hinges on our sensitivity for the individual. We pay close attention to what individuals want so we can know when, where, and how they will allow us to have a relationship with them. In order to succeed, we *must* apply this same sensitivity toward each other. If the silos of brand, direct, and sales can respect what each brings to the process, we all win.

Empathy is the cornerstone of convergence. Each department provides what the other needs. Brand builders, in all their creative glory, and direct folks, with their drive and accountability, can design campaigns to influence behavioral change in real time. We can reach individuals with programs that deliver results and *also* meet the financial demands of the business. Thus, you have this simple equation:

The best of brand + the best of direct + sales, powered by finance = success.

Hold that thought.

The Fine Art of Balancing Brand and Direct

Think about a music ensemble. Each musician has a specific role to play. Take away any one of them and the music would be lacking. Play the wrong part, and the music sounds odd, disharmonious. But if each musician plays his or her part with respect for the other musicians, the music goes beyond the science of theory and the technical skills of each player. It is transcendent. The ensemble plays, and we are moved, filled with emotion, enjoyment, and gratitude. The ensemble works because everyone does his or her part, harmoniously, toward the shared goal. The harmonious convergence of brand and direct is a fine art and, when tuned, can be played successfully, with all media and channels working in harmony.

So how do we get there? Baby steps. We need to take small steps within the existing marketing process. Ideally, the highest level of the organization would champion the convergence of marketing, advertising, sales, IT, and finance to work together. They would change the reward structure, making it beneficial for the culture to change. And they would review other changes that can support the new culture. But we can't wait for them to write that memorandum. Nope, we need to get things started *now*—with a change of mind-set.

Years ago, the National Aeronautics and Space Administration (NASA) cultivated a culture that landed a man on the moon. Everyone who worked there, from the top techno-heads to the cleaning lady, believed that he or she was working toward a common goal: to get a man on the moon. But, naturally, it required more than just believing. Getting a man on the moon required teamwork, knowledge, technology, engineering, and so on. And the day Neil Armstrong took "one giant leap for mankind," they all celebrated their success. The good news is we're not talking rocket science! This will be easy.

Our common language of respect is achieved through empathy. Think of a headline that comes from the heart. Can you see how this begins a meaningful relationship with the individual? We don't want to yell at individuals or demand a response we haven't earned. So, touch the clients, show them you care. Don't tell them. Listen to them—with total respect and sensitivity. Not overstepping our bounds and working from a place of empathy and respect is our most important consideration as we design the copy, graphic, and offer. Reaching out with empathy is critical in today's marketing and advertising environment.

What We Know and Why It Matters

Let's take a deeper look at what each part of the equation brings to convergence. The best brand builders give us those indelible images that instantaneously connect us to the brand. They create the iconic symbols of our day for everything from laptops to running shoes, and they create those magical jingles we cannot get out of our heads. They study our psychology and our psyche. They know what colors pull us in, fire us up, and turn us on. And on their best days, they leave us wanting more. Leo Burnett said it best: "Good advertising does not just circulate information. It penetrates the public mind with desires and belief."[1]

Brand builders are the artful masters of awareness. When they do their job right, the slightest hint of provocation brings their creation immediately to mind. Think about the Nike swoosh, the rainbow-striped Apple, the Golden Arches, and the famous Marlboro Man. Brilliant stuff.

---

[1]Leo Burnett, "BrainyQuote,"

Direct marketers are exactly that—direct. They get to us where we live, with messages that make us want to respond to an artful call to action, and begin a meaningful dialogue. They are the masters of change, using information to change the *behavior*, not just the attitude, of the individual. They can strategically initiate and develop a relationship through a one-on-one dialogue and, in doing so, feel the pulse of the individual. Then they can track and measure both the success and the cost of their relationship. They have developed tools that move the individual forward in the sales process, and they can determine the pacing of that step so as not to freak anyone out by moving too fast. After all, they want a long-term relationship, to sell and resell to the same individuals over time, because an essential part of their craft is to work with the sales team to move product. After all, our job is to make money for our clients.

The current trend in marketing is to create an experience with the brand, and I'm all for it. We need to apply the tools of direct to create a relationship that fulfills the desire for that experience. Lester Wunderman, known to many as the father of direct advertising, saw it coming years ago. In his book *Being Direct*, he writes, "I believe that the successor to the brand image in the post-present will be the "brand-experience."[2]

Convergence brings brand and direct together in the same communications, the same messaging, the same print ads, commercials, e-mails, brochures, letters, and web sites. Combining the powerful knowledge, skills, and talents of these separate art forms is the next step in the evolution of our craft.

---

[2]Lester Wunderman, *Being Direct, Making Advertising Pay* (1971; repr., New York: Random House, 1996), 280.

Imagine a campaign that combines the artistry of brand with the personal connection of direct. Think beyond the visual. Look deeper into how the behavioral change agents of direct can get us to a one-on-one dialogue or experience. Imagine creating brand loyalty faster and stronger than ever before. This process is not as simple as sticking a toll-free number or web site on the corner of a print ad. It's about using the highly developed science of behavioral change agents, along with artful attention grabbing design, in a new way to achieve a shared goal.

Convergence begins with the common language of respect between direct and brand. Once we can respect each other's craft, we can begin to figure out the best way to combine and apply that knowledge to our shared goal. That goal is simple: create brand loyalty with the individual through an empathetic dialogue, thus creating profit for our clients. With our shared goal set, we can break through the old cultural silos and psychological barriers. This is the pathway to convergence.

3

CONVERGENCE

THE BEST OF BRAND + THE BEST OF DIRECT + SALES, POWERED BY FINANCE = SUCCESS

This simple equation is the foundation of convergence. We bring together the best ideas and techniques that connect us to the individual, so that we can communicate with the individual on his or her terms. For over 20 years, I've studied, tested, and developed this methodology. It is the fastest way to create brand resonance and build brand loyalty. We have all the tools we need right at our fingertips to reach the individual and build an empathetic relationship.

Today, it is all about respecting the individual. Convergence retains the powerful imagery and messaging of brand advertising while leveraging the motivational techniques of direct marketing, and focusing all of it on the goals set by sales. It is powered by a financial model, using the contribution margin of what the customer is expected to be worth in a set period of time. It is about making money fast; it happens in real time with statistics to guide the way; and it has the advantage of being a process we can repeat over and over again, as well as proving critical path accountability to the CFO. All parties know what should be done and what is a questionable use of precious resources—and they know it immediately, not six months after the fact. In the end, convergence drastically reduces business risk. The political machine is appeased, and the results and respective profits are rewarding for all. Sound too good to be true? I guess today must be your lucky day because it is true, and I'm going to tell you how to do it.

Convergence is a bit like Chemistry 101. We need to mix the right elements to get the expected reaction. So we're going to start by using the same basic elements we work with everyday to create a new combination and achieve a very different result.

The Best of Brand

The first key ingredient in convergence is *brand building*. Brand is the heart and soul of the company. Over the years, brand builders have developed a science that pulls us into a love affair with the brand. The aura of the brand—what we like or dislike about it—is everything. Brand builders create emotional excitement through imagery, jingles, and mouth-watering messages. They understand how to create desire and grow loyalty for the brand.

Brand builders know exactly what to do or say to create need and desire in their target buyer. Some targets are huge—I mean, didn't *everyone* desire the iPhone? And some targets are small, like me needing that really cool fiberglass sea kayak. Think back to the NASA story. Everyone embraced it, lived it, took ownership of it, and was motivated by it. Why? Because the brand message was clear, concise, and communicated.

We know that brands are more successful when we have an experience with them that is consistent with the brand persona. Convergence creates experiences and dialogue with the brand in order to strengthen brand loyalty.

One of the most valuable tools we need from branding to do our job well is a brilliantly crafted *brand brief*. It is also known as the *brand book* or *brand identification platform*. If we want all communications to reflect the essence, tone, and character of the brand, then it seems reasonable to have a brief that defines all of these intimate details with some emotion. It is essential that the brand brief sets this information in stone. And I am not referring to that corporate binder that defines the graphic guidelines. I'm talking about defining of the heart and soul, the hooks for the emotional link, the thing that makes us smile. We need to have a well-written brand brief to do our job well. Anything less gives us room for interpretation, creating our own definition, which results in weakening the brand.

The Best of Direct

The second key ingredient in convergence, *direct marketing*, is the science of moving people forward in the sales process, either to interaction/leads or to sales. Direct marketers know how to measure and project every possibility. They can push the limits of interaction and build brand using every kind of media available, in ways that traditional advertising can barely fathom. We need to move beyond the idea that direct means direct mail. In fact, direct marketing is, and has always been, about getting people to move forward in the sales process. You see it in every advertisement that asks you to respond, like a television commercial that tells you to call an 800 number, or a web banner with a link to some product you want to check out. I like to think of it as building communications via any media to provide prospects and customers with "proof of concept points" for their consideration. Some of the general agencies are behaving as though they just discovered some of the very tools that direct marketers have used and perfected over the past 30 years. Look at the viral programs that are so hip today. They were born out of a 30-year old technique direct marketing folks call *continuity programs*, like the Book-of-the-Month Club. The *interactive experience* branding companies are incorporating into the marketing of their products, stores, and web sites was invented by direct marketers. I see it as a positive indication that brand and direct need each other to optimize their effect and stretch their budgets. If you're a frustrated brand builder, rather than wasting time and energy trying to invent new tools, why not take one of your direct marketing coworkers to lunch? There are so many preexisting solutions, and if it makes you feel better you can give the old direct marketing solution a cool new name.

The Best of Sales

Combining the best of brand and direct is starting to make sense, as both have proven skill sets that can enhance the objective of the other. But what the heck does *sales*, our third ingredient, have to do with it? As a matter of fact, the idea for this methodology was inspired by my experience in sales and challenged during my early experiences in direct and brand marketing. I can assure you that sales has a great deal to do with it because salespeople are the "eyes of the corporation." Salespeople are on the frontline every day—listening, probing, questioning, and then answering the customers' hard questions. They know why someone likes or doesn't like, trusts or doesn't trust, buys or doesn't buy. They hone their craft, staying on top of every new version of the products, training in the latest sales techniques the corporation supports while learning the new marketing materials. With ever-increasing competition and complexity in the market, the need to support them with real-time information is more critical today than ever before.

One of the tools we need to learn from sales is called *objection selling*. Rather than focusing our strategy and creative on features and benefits, we need to know why an individual *wouldn't* move forward—the individual's potential objections. In the new world of convergence marketing, we'll create objection messaging maps to outline the objections and barriers to purchase. We will seek to understand and overcome those objections in our communications. We use this information to enrich our presentation of features and benefits to quickly gain favor in the heart of the individual. Objection selling gives everyone in marketing and advertising the right perspective to develop the empathetic dialogue needed at each phase of the sales process.

Not only can we benefit from their frontline knowledge of the customer, but also we can gain some serious traction from their database. Sales organizations use sales support software to isolate and define customers, lovingly referred to as the *pipeline*. Convergence uses the same idea, relying on a database to methodically build relationships and communicate with customers. It works for both consumer and business-to-business (B-to-B) marketing. The pipeline has been a sales tool for as far back as I can remember. We are going to use the database to understand exactly where the individual is in the sales process so we can communicate directly to the individual. From now on, everyone in marketing and advertising will understand that a fulfillment package sent to a prospect is not merely fulfillment, but another important step in the sales process. Internalizing this new information will help us determine the next step for each customer, as well as the communication needed to get the customer there.

The Power of Finance

It's the cringe heard 'round the planet—after all, most creatives don't do math. But we are in business, after all, and finance drives everything in business. There is no way to avoid it, but you won't need to anymore—I can assure you that this vital element of convergence will make your life richer. Finance measures our short- and long-term success. Let's focus on the expenditures of marketing and advertising programs across the enterprise. We need to look at the current setup so we can see how these programs may need to be reconfigured to help you gain market share. You need to be able to present your ideas to a CFO in the language he understands.

Convergence uses finance to determine the appropriate investment *spend* as well as the expected value of the individual. We use differential accounting, the process of burdening only the direct cost of goods sold and overhead, as a new source of funds to invest in future marketing and advertising. Rather than trying to estimate the lifetime value of the individual, we'll take a more pragmatic approach and project the *expected value over a set period of time*. This could be as short as a few months or as long as several years.

Most folks determine their marketing and advertising costs based on a percentage of sales from this year's static profit and loss. Working that way is about as precise as pulling a number out of a hat. Convergence uses a much more efficient model based upon real-time accounting. By gathering information from an individual after the transaction, we can determine his or her worth. Using the power of statistics, we'll arrive at weighted averages for sales and costs that we can trust. We'll understand the contribution margin to profit and use that knowledge to drive marketing and advertising costs. In other words, you'll work with actual, proven statistics that relate to sales to build a model that works for years to come.

A Short Story

A few years ago, I was on a business flight and happened to be seated next to the VP of finance for Motorola. We struck up a conversation about advertising and branding. Before I knew it, we were in a deep discussion about his brand executive's push to invest serious money into a strategic branding initiative called *digital DNA*. The VP shared his frustration over the brand person's attempt to justify the huge cost, citing successful campaigns such as "Intel inside" to support his argument. The VP wanted to invest, but the tangible benefits of market share did not outweigh the investment. However, had the brand exec been able to speak to the financial benefits, the return on the investment in the short- and long-term, he would have succeeded. He needed the tools of convergence.

GETTING STARTED WITH CONVERGENCE

In a research study completed by the Direct Marketing Association (DMA) in May of 2007,[1] seasoned professionals agreed that interacting with an individual early in the sales process works better. The results improved with the combination of media.

Over the years I've seen how convergence stimulates the creative team to find a more emotional and empathetic execution of the communications. It gets us to the heart of the matter and is more engaging than just driving someone to awareness. Using the power of heartfelt headlines with great visuals, convergence communications are strategically designed to move the individual forward in the sales process, right now. Understanding where the individual is in the sales process is crucial. Not overstepping our bound is paramount. Oftentimes, the messaging uses a problem-solution platform. And, more often than not, there is a solid call to action. Convergence uses more copy than a traditional awareness ad in order to set the stage for both short- and long-term time frames.

I'm going to walk you through an overview of convergence. Once you have this general understanding of the methodology, I'll provide much deeper insight into each aspect. You'll also be given pragmatic tools and case studies to help you move forward with this practical and timely approach to marketing and advertising. Following in Figure 3.1 is a helpful comparison between

---

[1] *The Integration of DM & Brand* (New York: Direct Marketing Association, 2007).

Figure 3.1   Traditional Model versus Brand-Interaction

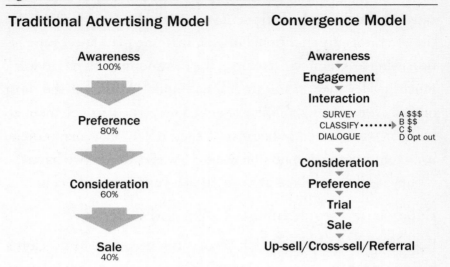

the traditional model that still works for a few and the new model of Brand-Interaction that is proven to work with high yield and leverage for many.

Phase One: *Awareness to Interaction*

We begin with awareness, just like the traditional model of classic advertising. Both models rely on the creative to set the stage for the brand and stop the individual in their tracks. However, convergence is designed to drive the individual through not one, but three levels of communication, from *awareness* to *engagement* to *interaction*.

I want to get individuals to raise their hands, right away, by living and breathing the concept. If I treat them with respect, and communicate with empathy, they will raise their hands sooner than if I speak in broad strokes. Treat individuals the same way you would like to be treated. Show them that you care by using copy that is pleasant and honest. We will be able to move them through all three levels, with the same budget and time frame as the traditional model. Imagine that, faster interaction using less money. Of course, the communication has to work much harder than in the traditional model. We'll get the most out of every precious dollar spent. The goal is to get them to interact with us today because if they don't, they may not be back tomorrow—and no one wants to waste, nor do we have the money it takes, to chase after them like yesteryear.

Balance of Target, Image, Copy, and Offer

Beginning with the attraction phase, it is necessary to develop a balance of the four variables; target, image, copy, and offer, all coming together at the right time to attract and move the individual forward. The target needs to be clear, the images need to pull the individual in, the copy needs to be empathetic, and the offer needs to make sense. These factors, in perfect balance, will resonate with the individual and must be consistent throughout every phase of our communication.

While the traditional model used frequency to drive success, we're going to use *empathy*, a sensitive and powerful communication style, to generate *engagement*. Empathy is going to drive the communication to deliver greater traction and stimulate a response for the individual to get involved with the brand. We're going to deliver the brand attributes while turbo-charging the interaction rate of the communication. The creative must look good and perform with far more leverage. When it all works together, everyone will feel okay about building brand and demand at the same.

Phase Two: Compressing the Sales Cycle

We've designed the communication to build brand and demand at the same time. We're using the same budgets that would have gone toward just awareness. Now we're ready to nurture the relationship. Respect for the individual is paramount for both short- and long-term success. Nurturing has been referred to as *permission* or *relationship marketing*.

Based upon individuals' initial interaction with us, we're going to ask them a few probing questions, similar to what a good salesperson would do. Most important, we need to keep it simple and non-threatening. We want to know how they feel about things, but we're not going to try to close them right away. We simply want to find out more about them and their level of interest. We want to learn about them so we can determine where they are in the sales cycle.

The way the copy is written and the questions presented will determine whether individuals will interact, so we better get it right. I may ask some "pain-oriented" questions, like what itch they want to scratch, rather than asking what product or service they want to buy. At the same time, too many questions will irritate individuals. Think about those online surveys that never end. Few of us ever go beyond question nine. I recommend no more than five.

Years ago, I had the pleasure of working with a dynamic marketing manager to launch a new version of software. In one meeting, she asked this poor marketing guy, "Why the heck would you want to ask that question now? You can ask it later." She was right. If it's something you can ask at a later date, then wait.

The rule is, never ask a question that doesn't affect the initial dialogue sequence. Questions that err on the side of "too soon" assume purchase rather than consideration, such as What color or size do you want, or how many? Do you want to lease or buy? In some cases you can lose up to 20 percent of your response for each question you ask too soon. Be careful. Don't ask additional questions that won't alter your response or investment path. It is powerful to know who is responding, but don't let your enthusiasm get the best of you. Empathy and sensitivity toward the individual is the best course of action.

How do we get the individuals to respond to our questions? We're going to reward them for taking the time by giving them something they want. It can be a guide, a delicious food item, some fun tchotchke, or a brilliant white paper. It has to be something that makes them feel appreciated. We gain the knowledge we need from their answers to take the next important step in our relationship with them. Using preset criteria, we can classify them into A, B, and C leads. So now we can dialogue with them one-on-one, with respect to where they are and their level of interest in us.

According to Jim Obermayer of Sales Linkage Consulting, "Within a year, on average, about 45% of inquiries buy from the advertiser or a competitor. We call it the 'rule of 45'"[2] If they're not buying from you, they're buying from your competition. With this in mind, how much should you spend to go after individuals who raised their hands but didn't connect or get closed by one of your salespeople within that 30-day period? The best

---

[2]Bob Donath, James W. Obermayer, Carol K. Dixon, and Richard Crocker, *Managing Sales Leads: How to Turn Every Prospect into a Customer* (Lincolnwood, IL: NTC Publishing Group, 1996), 18.

way to lower your risk and deliver qualified prospects and leads to the sales team is to build long-term relationships that minimize customer attrition.

Phase Three: Consideration and Preference

The next phase of our overview of convergence is moving the individual to consideration and preference. This is where classic advertising wants to rush because this is where the rubber hits the road. Delivering more individuals into this phase with greater efficiency is something we only dreamed about in the 1990s. But now we have the technology to dialogue with finesse. Respecting our relationship with individuals opens new doors. Instead of pushing our communications at them, we reach out with empathy, from a place of respect. E-mail is one of the strongest technologies for dialogue when used with respect. Otherwise, it's called *spam*.

A few years ago, I worked with Bill Nussey, President of Silverpop and author of *The Quiet Revolution in Email Marketing*. Bill and his firm have mastered e-mail as a pragmatic dialogue vehicle for building customer databases. After all, the database is the engine behind any successful marketing machine. E-mail has transformed how we interact with the individual. Everyone in business today knows at least some of the attributes of this tremendous technology. This new generation of marketing tools, which include e-mail and the web, can turn soft exchanges into powerful relationships with exponential, (Return on Investment) ROI-driven sales, over time.

We have to be respectful during our dialogue to successfully move individuals forward into preference. After all, our goal is to get the individual to flow through the cycle, going from preference to consideration to trial, to sale, and back to up-sell, and to the cross-sell referral program. It all hinges on our initial interaction. The crucial shift in our behavior is that we are going to move this relationship forward at the individuals' speed. If we do our job correctly, there will be more than enough sales downstream. The A leads will give us the revenue for this quarter. The B leads, usually coming in at three to four times the volume of the As, will deliver the pipeline of relationships we need well into the following three quarters.

The magic of convergence is how to put these pieces together. That's the secret sauce. I've dedicated an entire chapter on it called "The Ask and The Offer." You'll see how some of the oddest combinations can deliver the highest yields.

Meet the Primary Drivers

These are four powerful primary concepts for you to employ with this new model. I will touch on them here and expand on them in upcoming examples and case studies.

Know and respect the brand. This is the golden rule. You must know the essence of the brand and how it resonates in everything about the brand. It's what you stand for every time you talk about the company, in every communication you craft, and every time you answer the phone.

Target the individual where they are in the sales cycle with messages that resonate. Specific messages are designed to speak to individuals at precise points within the sales cycle. We use all media, creating options for them to talk with us in the way that is most comfortable for them, whether it's via web, mail, or phone.

Combine the disciplines to influence behavioral change in real-time. The fusion of brand, direct, and sales gives us greater perspective for understanding the individuals and their behaviors, thus providing greater opportunity for us to interact with them and influence behavioral change.

Create a customer rather than a transaction. Historically, marketing and sales operate in short-term thought. You can see it in those industries that push for the fast sale, the quick fix, such as insurance and auto dealerships. However, when we treat the individual like a transaction rather than a person, millions of dollars are left on the table because we kill the long-term potential. Instead, we need to nurture that potential by creating a relationship.

For me, finding balance with my communications has been my life's work. We must have the shared goal and come to the table with a common language. We need to fine-tune our organizations so we can get the most out of all our resources, and we need a tool that defines and drives the goal of the communication for all to see. That tool is called the Rosen Velocity Scale.™

II

MEASURING THE INTENTION AND SUCCESS: PROCESS TOOLS AND PRACTICAL APPLICATIONS

4

ACCELERATE AND DRIVE
The Rosen Velocity Scale™

The Rosen Velocity Scale is a business process tool used to drive and measure the speed with which the communication stimulates an interaction between the individual and the brand. It can be applied to all media. That's right; we can actually tune the assertiveness of any communication to the level of interaction we want it to have with the individual. Using this tool allows us to strategically plot out the desired velocity for each communication in a campaign that uses multiple media and predetermine the speed of interaction for each piece of the campaign. We then measure to see if we achieved the anticipated planned results.

There is a lot more to this than meets the eye, or ear, for that matter. Designing an advertisement to meet the desired result requires a specific balance of image, copy, offer, and target. Each

Figure 4.1   The Rosen Velocity Scale

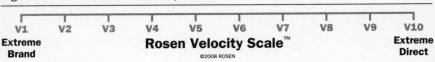

element affects the pull of the ad and must be critically considered to achieve the predetermined result. Please see Figure 4.1. Have fun, for many a person after a speech has walked up to me and simply said, "Thank you. You have saved me years." As you go through it, think about what it looks like in print and how you might adapt it for all other media.

The scale goes from V1 to V10. The far left, at V1, represents Extreme Brand. At the opposite end of the scale, V10 represents Extreme Direct. So the opposite ends of the scale represent the extremes of each discipline. With our new goal of balancing brand and direct to achieve a predetermined result, we need to look toward the center. It seems obvious that we need to be centered to have balance in our communication. So it is at V5, the middle of the scale, where we will create more interaction with the individual while showing equal respect for the brand.

The Visual Manifestation of the Goal

One of the things I love most about the scale is that it is the visual manifestation of the goal of the communication. Everyone, from marketing and advertising to sales, IT, and finance can see it, and, therefore, it provides a basis for our common language. Everyone understands the intention and goal of the communication.

The scale can be used to define the level of communication with the client, the product managers, and literally everyone throughout the company. And not only can you use it to clarify the visual media, but also you can use it to set the expectations for each medium.

We're not using it to measure the effectiveness of the creative; we are using it to measure the velocity of the interaction. The design of the ad must use the elements of image, copy, design, and offer to create the desired velocity of the communication. To help us design the communication, we need to consider the tone, the behavioral change agents, and how it all comes together to move the individual forward at our predetermined speed.

It is important to understand that we can build brand and demand anywhere along the scale and create communications that drive awareness, to engagement, to interaction. We need to create ads that work harder than ever, and now we have the tools to help us do so.

How the Scale Works

On the extreme left, at V1, we have the pure brand-awareness ads, also known as the *big idea*—like Nike's "Just Do It" ads. The ad is designed to catch the attention of the individuals and create a favorable attitude in their minds. In the category of new products, the idea is to link the product closely to its existing category so that the brand name becomes synonymous with the product. Perfect examples of this are Levi's, Coke, Kleenex, and Xerox. Awareness advertising is all about the big picture, the broad spectrum. This is where the general advertising agencies make their living, win their awards, and often wow us with brilliant ideas.

Most of traditional advertising sits in this first quadrant, between V1 and V3 on the scale, emulating brand awareness campaigns. However, most companies don't have the large budget to drive the necessary frequency to gain complete mind share of the individual. These ads are not designed for interaction or response. This is why many campaigns fall short of what they could have accomplished, great on creative, but short on velocity and profit.

As we move toward the center of the scale, there are several key issues that I need to clarify. First of all, the velocity does not equate with budget because it's based upon interaction rather than frequency. Therefore, we design an ad to spark interaction. We don't need to run it a bazillion times to get it into their heads to gain mindshare. Second, we are going to quantify the ad into a specific place on the scale so that we are all clear on what we want the ad to achieve. A lot of creative directors will throw up their hands and tell you it's not possible to quantify the creative process. But I can assure you it is. I've been doing it for years.

Now we move to the middle of the scale, centered at V5, which represents the balance of both extremes. Moving away from the pure awareness ads toward the middle of the scale creates more interaction with the individual while still respecting the brand. V5 respects the brand while incorporating strategies and tactics from both sales and direct to get the individual to interact with you faster, using less money.

However, as you move further right, toward Extreme Direct, at about V9, you have reached the epitome of short-term sales.

Terms like "Buy Now!" and "Free-Offer!" compromise the brand. The least amount of money is spent, and high velocity is achieved, but it is done at the expense of the brand.

SURE, BUT WILL IT FLY? CRITERIA FOR THE ROSEN VELOCITY SCALE

Just like any great idea, the general concept is intriguing, but do we have the scientific proof that it will do the job it's meant to do? It's like Orville and Wilbur Wright pondering over blueprints in their efforts to fly. Sure, they were smart, had a really nice bicycle shop, and hung out with some of the most brilliant inventors of their day. But I'm sure a lot of folks scratched their heads. Sure, it looks good on paper—but will it fly?

I can assure you this machine flies. The scale is a great tool for the common language, and the science involved is specific. If you follow it, you will achieve the velocity you intend. And what could be better than designing an ad to do a specific job and seeing it do exactly that?

I'm going to walk through the criteria using print ads from TaylorMade Golf. I did some work with TaylorMade back in the late 1990s, and these ads do a great job of taking us through each step. It's important to note that we started with the gorgeous awareness ad from their general agency, Foot Cone Belding, and built upon it to show the full spectrum of the scale from V1 through V10. These ads never ran, but they perfectly illustrate the function and criteria for print advertising.

The first ad (see Figure 4.2) began the campaign. It sits at V1 on the scale and is a pure brand awareness ad designed to build

Figure 4.2   TaylorMade Ad V1

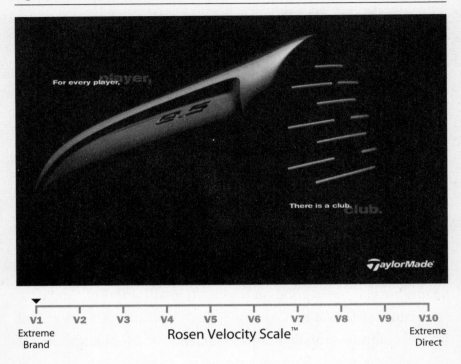

awareness. It is designed for long-term brand building. The ad is 100 percent brand and 0 percent direct or interaction. Because of the wide range of creativity in advertising, each piece of the criteria will not be presented in every print ad. However, the criteria are general guidelines for a preponderance of criteria that indicate where the ad sits on the Velocity Scale. In this ad, you can see that simplicity is paramount. Only one message is presented, in a clean, elegant, and uncluttered way, with minimal copy. There is no attempt to interact, no call to action, no offer, nor any other device that detracts from the power of the concept.

The following are criteria for a successful V1 print ad:

Headline	0 to 8 words
Subheads	None
Body copy	1 to 100 words
Call to action	None
Image complexity	Simple
Number of messages	1
Degree of message substantiation	Low
Offer	None
Graphic response elements	None

A V2 is 90 percent brand and 10 percent direct (see Figure 4.3). Branding is still extremely important, but we're going to spark a response. The differences between a V1 and V2 are very small.

Figure 4.3   TaylorMade Ad V2

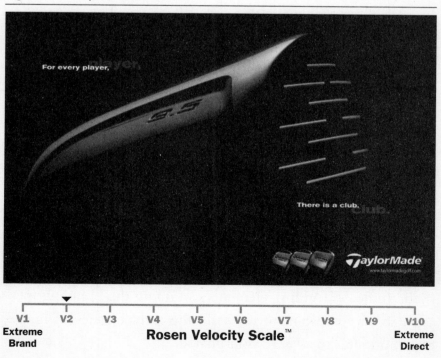

We've added a web site to the lower right corner, directly under the logo, and we've added a small image of golf club heads to the same area. These elements will pull minor response and are aligned with the goal of a V2, which is to start interaction and lead generation rather than engaging a sale. The ad does reach out to the individual with a mechanism to communicate directly with the company to obtain more information. This can be done by way of a toll-free number or a web site address, as we've done, and simply adding that information is a minimum response technique. This subtle approach pulls poor response and might get a few A leads to react. Adding the word *call* will increase the response; "Call for more information" will increase response even higher, and adding the word *free*, as in "Call for free information," will get an even higher response.

There are a number of ways to say *free*, and each has a different level of response. The softer terms, such as *no cost*, are more aligned with branding, especially if the product is more sophisticated. However, the word *free* is preferable in most cases. The more you draw attention to the word, the higher the response. *FREE* will pull a higher response than *free*. Of course, this is predicated on the free offer being something desirable to your target.

Adding call-to-action words to the copy increases the interaction of the ad, while increasing the brand awareness aspect as well. Keep in mind that you are adding a second message. So your goal must be well-defined before you start designing and writing the copy for your ad, so as to diminish the feeling of aesthetic trade-off. Adding elements can dilute the branding message, so it's important to maintain the right balance of image, copy, and offer to achieve your goal.

The following are criteria for a successful V2 print ad:

Headline	0 to 10 words
Subheads	0 to 2
Body copy	1 to 150 words
Call to action	800 number, web site, e-mail, etc.
Image complexity	Less simple
Number of messages	1
Degree of message substantiation	Low
Offer	Rare
Graphic response elements	None

The changes from V1 to V2 are very subtle, but they make a difference in the overall performance of the ad.

As we move further to the right of the scale, we up the ante on interaction with the individual. Moving to a V3 (see Figure 4.4),

Figure 4.4   TaylorMade Ad V3

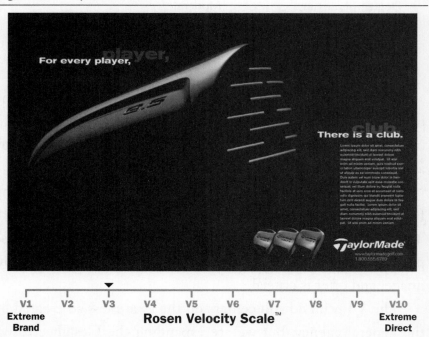

we are at 80 to 70 percent brand and 20 to 30 percent interaction. You will most likely have an increase in body copy because there is a need to give more information to engage the individual to interact. In addition to the expansion of copy, we have a change in the overall appearance of the ad. Depending upon the strength of the brand, we want to make the call to action stronger. We can add a graphic element to draw attention to an offer, deadline, or some new idea being introduced.

The following are criteria for a successful V3 print ad

Headline	1 to 14 words
Subheads	2 to 4
Body copy	50 to 200 words
Call to action	Bold 800 number, web site, e-mail, etc.
Image complexity	Moderate
Number of messages	1 or more
Degree of message substantiation	Moderate
Offer	Sometimes
Graphic response elements	0 to 1

The V3 print ad may not have the elegance of a V1, but the brand is still very strong. What it does achieve quite well is to initiate a response through the right balance of additional copy and a bolder call to action.

Before I move forward, it is important to note that moving further to the right isn't really about throwing in a bunch of stuff. This is the mistake most people make when looking at these print ads at face value. The balance of placement of the copy, image, and offer is crucial.

The V4 print ad still centers on the awareness ad created by the general agency, but we are expanding the Gestalt creative with an offer of golf balls, creating a stronger call to action and a glimpse of the product (See Figure 4.5). The ad is 60 percent brand and 40 percent interaction. And we are clearly moving into a dual-purpose ad, which is not flashy; that's not its purpose. A V4 is designed to build and maintain the brand while driving a response, an interaction with the brand.

An offer is the key element that differentiates a brand ad and a direct ad. A pure brand awareness ad, or a V1, is devoted to improving individuals' attitude toward the product. However, in a V4, we are concerned with both improving their attitude and changing their behavior so they will respond to us. It has to perform this double duty. It has to look good enough to enhance

Figure 4.5   TaylorMade Ad V4

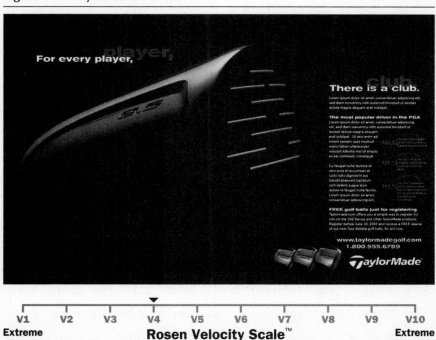

the brand perception while including response mechanisms to move the target to interact.

To borrow a truism from the direct playbook, one of the best ways to trigger a response is with an offer. Offers trigger the emotional motivator in the mind of the individual. The reaction to a V1 is "That looks good. I'll try that sometime." On the other hand, the reaction to a V4 is "That's a good idea, and I better call today to get the free golf balls." Face it; we all want a deal. We all love getting something for free. And a great offer works both sides of the brain. Golf balls trigger the emotional right brain, and free works with the rational left brain—so a response is in the bag.

The following are criteria for a successful V4 print ad:

Headline	1 to 16 words
Subheads	2 to 4
Body copy	100 to 250 words
Call to action	Bold 800 number, web site, e-mail, etc.
Image complexity	Moderate
Number of messages	1 or more
Degree of message substantiation	Moderate
Offer	Often
Graphic response elements	0 to 2

Because the body copy is longer, there is a need for two to four subheads to break the copy into easier-to-read sections. This enhances skimability and readability. The call to action is very clear, and the 800 number is in bold, making it easy to locate. The longer body copy also leaves less room for the image. Making the image smaller will eliminate crowding. There needs to be space to give flow to the ad. The overall effect is a more complex-looking ad that is trying to accomplish more than one thing. Multiple products might be shown or multiple uses of a single product. Each of the elements must support and substantiate the messages being presented.

A V4 usually has an offer with a time or quantity limit. This can range from sending the prospect more information, to special price offers, or to even costly premiums. The purpose is to increase the probability of response, or increase the interaction. By offering something that carries a certain perceived value, you can pull in the prospects who are sitting on the fence, either short term or long term.

Ah, finally we have reached the midpoint, the center, the perfect balance of brand and direct working harmoniously within the ad (see Figure 4.6). Neither one is dominating. Both are working to complement each other. I know; it sounds like Nirvana, which it can be if both extremes stay focused on the goal. The key is to compromise and everyone wins. We are creating the perfect blend of 50 percent brand and 50 percent direct, so this is far from business as usual. Phrases like, "But that's the way we've always done it" are not part of the dialogue.

V5 works best when you have a strong brand and your objective is to increase leads or sales. As you can see in the Taylor-Made example, we maintain the sexy product shot of an awareness ad, but we are emphasizing the aura of brand with a product hero shot that displays the logo within the product. Following the natural pull of the eye, starting at the left and landing on the right side of the page, we have plenty of copy. We reverse the black and white into a clean column, to focus on the benefits

Figure 4.6   TaylorMade Ad V5

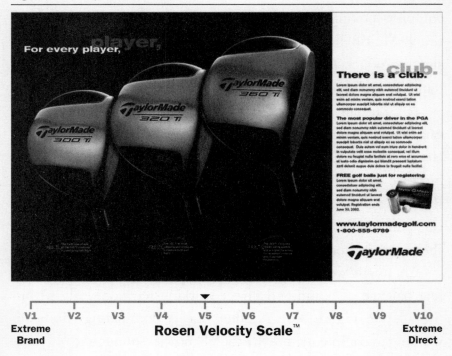

of the product, its popularity within the Professional Golfers' Association of America (PGA), and so on. And there is an offer that goes right to the sweet spot, FREE golf balls. That's right, just for calling. What golfer can turn down free golf balls? The copy is broken up into small sections, what I call skimability and readability. They can quickly skim through the copy by reading the subheads to capture the key points and understand the crux of it. They can choose to read the sections that interest them. Ideally, they will be pulled to take a moment and read all the copy, which is easy to get through in short order. The offer pops; we even added a picture of the offer to make sure we stop them from flipping past the ad.

The following are criteria for a successful V5 print ad:

Headline	2 to 18 words
Subheads	2 to 6
Body copy	200 plus words
Call to action	Bold 800 number, web site, e-mail, etc.
Image complexity	Moderate
Number of messages	1 or more
Degree of message substantiation	High
Offer	Always
Graphic response elements	0 to 2

As you can see in the criteria, the shift to interaction increases incrementally in several categories. The headline can be longer, and there might be several subheads. The copy is maybe around 200 or more words with a high degree of message substantiation. There is always an offer at V5 and at least one graphic element. Branding is present, usually in the logo and type, but not the dominant feature as in the previous ads to the left of center on the scale.

Moving one step to the right of center, the elements of direct become dominant (see Figure 4.7). Clearly the goal has a stronger interaction leading to sales emphasis. At V6, we are at 40 percent brand and 60 percent direct. We are more concerned with changing the individual's immediate behavior than his or her attitude over time. We still need to convey a reasonable degree of branding, but it is clear that the objective is to get the cash register to ring.

Additional branding efforts, such as public relations and great products and services, should collectively have an impact on

Figure 4.7   TaylorMade Ad V6

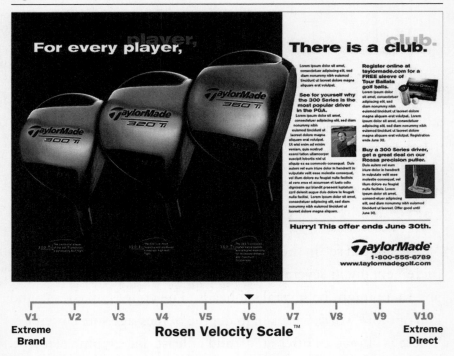

changing the individual's attitude for the short and long term—
in which case, we are free to move forward with changing their
behaviors, moving them from being passive readers to active
responders. We achieve this by integrating more interactive elements into the communication.

The following are criteria for a successful V6 print ad:

Headline	3 to 20 words
Subheads	2 to 6
Body copy	200 plus words
Call to action	Dominant 800 number, web site, e-mail, etc.
Image complexity	Very
Number of messages	1 or more

Degree of message substantiation	High
Offer	Often
Graphic response elements	1 or more

Although we have continued to use the same headline in our example, most ads will expand to a much longer headline in a V6 ad. The ad needs to pull us into the offer, and a longer headline can achieve this. And let's face it; some offers, because of their complexity, require more words. The subheads are made to pop out for two reasons. They break up the copy, and they emphasize more strongly the skimability and readability of the ad. Because our primary objective is selling, we usually need more copy, which means we have to shrink the images. At the same time, the images become more complex. The overall image is a bit busy, with less white space, but it is still aesthetically complimentary to the brand in a clean and orderly fashion. Each element plays a role in driving the individual toward interaction with the brand and is carefully crafted within the ad to achieve the maximum response. Again, it is not about adding more stuff. We have to keep in mind the behavioral elements, the way the eye moves from left to right and where it lands, the skimability and readability, along with images and offers that emotionally engage the individual.

V7 takes on a new look (see Figure 4.8). It is designed to lead beyond awareness to engagement and interaction, as opposed to ads that emphasize brand awareness. Notice that we've expanded the headline by adding a question, *"Which club is waiting for you?"* It will pull stronger to sales—after all, aren't you the golfer who deserves a great TaylorMade club? We are moving into stronger

Figure 4.8   TaylorMade Ad V7

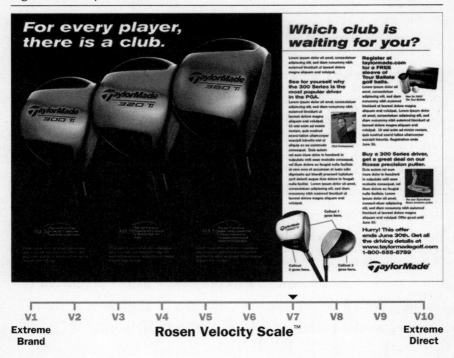

V1	V2	V3	V4	V5	V6	V7	V8	V9	V10

Extreme Brand   **Rosen Velocity Scale™**   **Extreme Direct**

direct tactics to support our goal of selling. At V7, the ad is 30 percent brand and 70 percent direct. Branding is greatly reduced to increase the response-generating techniques. Headlines are wordier, with more subheads and longer copy. We also have increased image complexity, with more photos that are technical in nature rather than the emotional photos used in pure branding ads.

The following are criteria for a successful V7 print ad:

Headline	4 to 22 words
Subheads	2 to 8
Body copy	200 plus words
Call to action	Dominant coupon, 800 number, web site, e-mail, etc.
Image complexity	Very

Number of messages	1 or more
Degree of message substantiation	High
Offer	Always
Graphic response elements	1 or more

In the TaylorMade V7 ad, we added a second offer, a deeply discounted putter in addition to the FREE golf balls. Why? They needed to unload putters and drivers to bring in the new models. We drove the offer with a deadline, "Hurry! This offer ends June 30." It's a great deal. Not only can you be the golfer you want to be with a TaylorMade club, but also you get a putter and the free balls you're going to need to work on that swing with your new driver. Sign me up!

A similar call to action is the use of a coupon. There is no better way to provoke interaction than with a coupon. The coupon works best in the lower right corner in order to capitalize on our conditioning. That's where we expect a coupon or call to action to be, at the end of a message presented in a left-to-right, top-to-bottom ad. Also, it is very important that a coupon look like a coupon. The art director needs to make a defined border that visually projects the appropriate behavior, which is to cut it out. Coupons trigger a strong desire for response. Some direct marketers will even create a coupon look around the toll-free number or web url to pull more response. It is a powerful tool that could be used when the need for response reaches the V7-plus level.

At V8 on the scale, we have a hard-hitting product ad, selling the clubs, the putter, and the offer (see Figure 4.9). The price is clearly outlined, and testimonials are added to build trust. This ad will pull higher response, but it also compromises the brand.

Figure 4.9　TaylorMade Ad V8

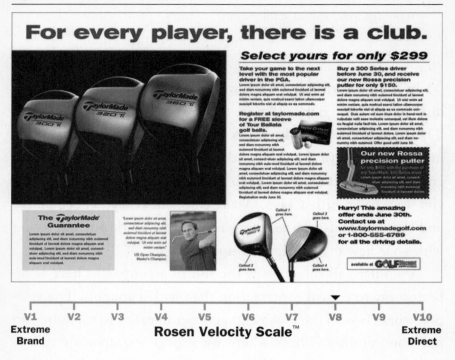

A V8 represents the right side of the scale. The velocity increases greatly, but it risks the integrity of the brand. The ad will pull tremendously over the response of a V1 to V3, but it falls under the *"Buy now!"* category and does not build brand with integrity over time.

A V8 is at 20 percent brand and 80 percent direct. The ad starts to look cluttered because we need to show either a lot of product or a lot of information or sales copy on a product.

The following are criteria for a successful V8 print ad:

Headline	5 to 24 words
Subheads	2 to 8

Body copy	250 plus words
Call to action	Coupon, 800 number, web site, e-mail, etc.
Image complexity	Cluttered
Number of messages	2 or more
Degree of message substantiation	Very high
Offer	Always
Graphic response elements	2 or more

There's no question looking over the criteria that we are on the extreme direct side of the scale. We are trying to convey two or more messages, so there is more copy to substantiate the messages, typically because, at this level, credibility is often an issue. Headlines, subheads, and body copy increase, so images and photos have to shrink to fit it all into the ad. V8 is about selling, no ifs, ands, or buts.

As we move further toward extreme direct, we are basically throwing brand out the window (see Figure 4.10). If your art director was unhappy with your request to create a V4 ad, they will freak out when you ask them to create a V9 ad. Hopefully, for your sake, you have an art director who understands the art of direct. These ads are packed with information and persuasive selling copy that are designed to overcome objections and skepticism. But nobody is going to win an award for a V9 ad. At 10 percent brand and 90 percent direct, the game is selling, with only a small element of brand, such as the logo, as a trust factor. The logo assures that the ad is from the trusted brand, and no one is going to get ripped off by interacting with the brand. The logo guarantees the information is supported by the reputation of the company.

Figure 4.10   TaylorMade Ad V9

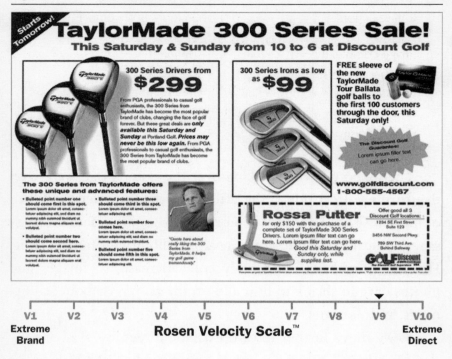

In our TaylorMade V9 example, we've locked in trust with the TaylorMade Guarantee. Plus, we have the endorsement of a pro golfer. So you know that these are not knockoffs but the top-of-the-line product that every golfer wants to own. We've altered the coupon, which is now linked to a national chain. So you know you can head right on over to the store in your area and get this great offer right away. The coupon is in the bottom right corner, the last place your eye will stop.

But up at the top of the ad we start with the push to sales. You have to come in this weekend, bring your coupon, and take advantage of these great deals. The FREE golf balls only go to the first 100 customers! After all, we need to move these clubs to make room for the new stock arriving on Monday.

Ads at this extreme right of the scale are often at the retail level where lots of different products need to be shown in a small space and the company needs to generate immediate sales.

The following are criteria for a successful V9 print ad:

Headline	6 to 26 words
Subheads	2 to 10
Body copy	250 plus words
Call to action	Coupon, 800 number, web site, e-mail, etc.
Image complexity	Cluttered
Number of messages	2 or more
Degree of message substantiation	Very high
Offer	Often
Graphic response elements	2 or more

Headlines can be as long as 26 words, and subheads can be up to 10. Body count is very long, except in the case of retail ads, like the ones for electronics, TVs, DVDs, and such that require a lot of product shots. And don't forget, prices may never be this low again!

We have now reached the point of no return. A V10 on the scale is high on velocity and nothing else (see Figure 4.11). It will move product. But you can forget the brand. It's not important. Besides, the folks who actually use this level of selling offer little to no value to most companies. V10s are most often used by obscure companies that sell fad products in a short span of time. One month they're selling the ultimate calorie counter, and the next month it's the amazing carrot peeler. There is no

Figure 4.11 TaylorMade Ad V10

V1	V2	V3	V4	V5	V6	V7	V8	V9	V10

Extreme Brand   **Rosen Velocity Scale™**   **Extreme Direct**

need for them to build a brand. They just want to move product.

In the V10 example, the logo is only visible on the product shots. We are selling everything, from drivers and putters to shoes. We have increased our tactics to bring you into the store so that we not only have the coupon and the FREE balls, but now we're offering the chance to meet a pro golfer!

I don't recommend going to this extreme in most cases. But it works when the goal is to move product. As for the brand— what brand? I actually prefer the use of a V9 over the V10. It will meet the sales goal while maintaining the integrity of the company.

The following are criteria for a successful V10 print ad:

Headline	7 to 28 words
Subheads	3 or more
Body copy	300 plus words
Call to action	Coupon, 800 number, web site, e-mail, etc.
Image complexity	Cluttered
Number of messages	2 or more
Degree of message substantiation	Very high
Offer	Always
Graphic response elements	Several

WHERE ARE YOU ON THE VELOCITY SCALE?

Knowing where you fit on the Rosen Velocity Scale requires a great deal of thought. You need to consider a few key factors:

- What is your present level of branding in comparison to your competitors?
- How strong is your brand in the marketplace?
- What percentage of your ad budget goes to increasing or maintaining your brand?
- Is your current placement on the scale and your balance of brand/direct appropriate for the products or service you are selling?
- What media are you using? Print? TV? Web? Mail? Social networks?
- Are your current ads primarily brand awareness? What other ads do you use?
- Are you achieving your intended results with your current campaigns?

- Most Important: Are you achieving the long-term brand and interaction goals to drive the level of business you and your management team need or want to deliver in today's global environment? If not, in general, please know you can increase your interaction rate via most media a minimum of three times. How exciting!

Over the past 20 years, I have found the scale to be a unifying tool with both clients and creative teams. It has allowed us to set clear objectives and provide better roadmaps to build communications via all media.

The first step is to critically understand where you are currently on the scale, and how you should go through the exercise with each communication and each medium you are using. From there, you need to determine where you want to be on the scale. And now the real work begins.

The Rosen Velocity Scale builds consensus on where you are and what you intend to build. It eliminates false starts and false promises of a communication. Instead of suddenly encountering the gap between the marketing plan and the campaign delivered, we can see if we're on target long before we fall into that gap. Agencies can use the scale as a pragmatic tool to deliver brilliant creative with an intended velocity.

All advertising needs to be brilliant, and we're going to use the same budget to build both brand and demand at the same time. For the same dollars it would cost to do just one, we will do both. Sure, it means dragging stubborn purists from either side with their heels dug in, who refuse to take a chance on yet another version of integrated marketing. But this is not a call for a blind leap of faith. Use the tools. Find consensus. Besides, it's fun to do something new and beneficial for all when you have tools and a proper roadmap. Right?

TESTING THE VELOCITY SCALE WITH THE BIG KIDS AT GENERAL MOTORS

A few years ago, I had the pleasure of teaching a seminar to the brand managers at General Motors (GM) University. For the purpose of the seminar, I selected their OnStar campaign for a number of reasons. I liked the empathy of the product, which went into many of their cars, so we weren't focusing on just one brand. We started with a print ad that was V2 on the scale. Good creative, but considering the budget cutbacks of the day, the double-page ad seemed excessive to me, considering it had very low leverage.

As part of the exercise, I showed them the same ad transformed into a V3, V4, V5, and V6, without making any major changes to the creative. The new ads would not only drive awareness, but also they would take the individual to engagement and interaction. Granted, not everyone liked what they saw. But they did see the power of convergence and the results it could deliver.

That afternoon, I broke everyone into small groups and gave them one problem to work on. The problem was this: What would you do with all of your media (print, TV, mail, e-mail, banners, organic/paid search web, etc.) to relaunch a very poor-selling brand of cars in the late stage of its product life cycle? We began by looking at what GM was doing at the time within each medium. We were able to substantiate that a budget of $15 million delivered 46,000 hard and soft leads—what I call *brand-interaction points* (BIPs). Everyone was disappointed to see how low the response rate was. So with this knowledge in hand, they went to work within their teams and proceeded to apply the new variable of velocity.

Armed with my Convergence Marketing Accelerator work-sheets, they proceeded to reallocate the budget. Their goal was to achieve a higher level of interaction rate in each medium by using a better balance of brand attributes and direct attributes. The results were amazing. These conservative brand managers sitting at nine round tables shared their strategies with the rest of the room. Each had their own rationale of why the Velocity Scale made so much sense and allowed them to rethink their strategy and budget, and each team was excited to report that they could increase the BIPs to 130,000 to 160,000 using the same budget of $15 million dollars. In short, rethinking the strategy for the budget by adding the new variable of velocity gave them a 300 percent increase. That's right, a 300 percent increase using the same budget.

We all sat back and said, "Wow." And then I asked the important question, "What did we lose by increasing the velocity?" After all, we need to understand the downside as well. In other words, we increased the velocity but at what cost to the brand? The overall response was that we were respectful of the brand, we did not compromise it, and we had achieved a better model for GM. Unfortunately, they realized that the existing culture would not rush to embrace the model because there are silos at stake.

REAL-TIME ACCOUNTABILITY AND THE KILLER APP

I was consulting with a client, a mattress manufacturer in the United States, who was competing in the space of new technology beds. Our efforts proved one of the most important variables of using the Velocity Scale, which is the ability to be accountable in real time. First of all, the scale helped us define the parameters with creative services. Second, it gave both brand and direct managers a way to see that they were on the same team. Each had similar goals of driving brand resonance and stimulating short-term sales to pay for and sustain a dynamic budget that would feed the media machine.

But the most important variable that came out of this experience was real-time accountability. The agency for the brand manager came up with a new creative campaign that the direct manager saw as too ethereal. Rather than having a debate over aesthetics, we went ahead with their new creative and built ads on the scale at V4 through to V8. The test resolved the debate for both the brand manager and the direct manager because the numbers were clear. The ads didn't pull well at all. No matter how we ran it, the response was extremely low. And we were able to see it, clearly, without politics or legacy silo behavior muddying our view. I think the vice president of marketing for the group nailed it when he called the Velocity Scale the "killer app."

The ability to know what your ad campaign is doing in real time is critical. You don't need to wait three to six months to find out what's going on. With some media, like the web, you can test overnight. Using the Velocity Scale can give your entire organization the ability to know what is working and what is not working.

And if it's not working to your liking, you can alter it or shut it off and move the budget to deliver better elsewhere. The Velocity Scale is a great tool to help us design the communication for our goal and target. Now we need to understand exactly where the target is located within the sales cycle.

I predict that this level of real-time accountability will help to bring print advertising back in vogue. After all, if we use the scale appropriately, a well-designed print ad can build brand and demand at the same time, the likes of which we have never before seen.

5

SALES CYCLE AND CUSTOMER DIALOGUE

One day you're walking down the street, and a total stranger who appears to be intelligent, attractive, and interesting stops and says "hello." If you're like me, you're struggling to remember who this person is. But then, out of nowhere, the person asks you to marry them. Now you're dumbstruck. Talk about bizarre. You don't even know who this person is. The person must be out of his or her mind, asking you to make such a huge commitment to a total stranger. You run away as quickly as possible in the opposite direction.

The sales process is no different than this scenario. We all need to go through a decision-making process that requires a certain amount of information before we reach a comfort level sufficient to act. Any advertiser or marketer worth his or her weight must understand the art of selling in order to do his or her job.

How Do We Decide What to Buy?

Countless textbooks, both business and psychological, have done in-depth studies of the variables that motivate us to buy. I'll touch on the key points you need to understand for our craft.

When faced with an ad for a new product, if the ad is doing its job, the first thing the ad will do is get your attention. It must be targeted to reach you, for example, by its location in a magazine or publication that you, as the target, would read. So this ad must use one of many techniques to stop you as you flip through the pages.

Once your eyes stop on the ad, you rapidly scan it. Part of your brain is stimulated by the newness of it, and the other part of your brain remembers past disappointments. Usually, the cautious side wins out the first time you see the ad, which is why we use repetition to wear you down. Or you can use the new tools of convergence and build a relationship with the brand through the use of offers to get you to dialogue with the brand, rather than pushing you into the commitment of purchase. Of course, buying a product that we are already familiar with is a much simpler process. Caution is down, and the ad just needs to convince you to buy this product now rather than later.

Television and the web have the advantage of appealing to our emotional side, increasing our desire for the product. We can see how much fun the product is and how it would make us cooler or make our life better. A 30- or 60-second spot or video pod is designed to entice you into buying now, blocking out the practical argument that you could probably wait. So we'll drive you to go to the phone or web site right now and order your very own, life-altering product. A good response commercial can block your logical mind by substituting replacement logic. In other words, you have logical justification that supports your emotional need for the product, and you're going to need it when your spouse finds out and accuses you of losing all sense. Television marketers know that they are dealing with an emotional sale and that passage of time, or a cooling-off period, will decrease sales. Video on the web will perform differently, however, the same characteristics hold true. That's why cash on delivery (COD) is not accepted. Experience has shown that by the time the product is delivered, many buyers will have changed their minds and refuse to accept the product and pay the COD.

However, our emotional and logical decision making is different when it comes to print ads. The emotional desire for the product is pitted against our present and future needs, available funds and projected income, and a vast array of complex factors that could include our feelings about the near-term economic outlook. This is why it's so important to research and understand the objections and interests of the target.

This all gets even more complicated as the price goes up. The average person is more reluctant to make an instant purchase because the level of commitment and risk accelerates proportionately to the price increase, as shown in Figure 5.1.

Figure 5.1 Purchase Price/Risk Relationship Chart

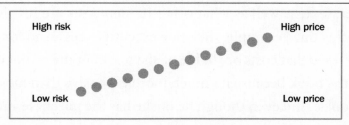

The Effects of Price and Risk

Clearly, the advertiser needs to be aware of where the product sits on this chart, so he or she can factor in the comfort level of the target, or individual. It's simple, and too often overlooked, to put the blame on the life of the product's sales cycle. Granted, price is one reason for a product's long sales cycle, but it's not always the case or reason.

Here are a few examples:

An executive sees an ad offering a "FREE DVD" that demonstrates the latest features of a $100,000 luxury car. He or she receives the DVD, views it, likes what he or she sees, and goes to the dealer to make the purchase. For the executive, the price and risk were low, he or she was already familiar and comfortable with the car and the manufacturer, and he or she chose to afford it.

In another example, the controller of the company the executive works for shows the executive an ad for a $100,000 piece of equipment that could save the company time and money in the production of their product. The executive will not consider the purchase until he or she has had a chance to research it. The reason is simple; there is a higher degree of risk. The executive needs to know if the company's competitors are using it, the item's proven success rate, the cost of training someone to operate it, as well as what other hidden costs are involved.

In this third example, the same executive sees an ad for a marketing book that costs $250. He or she tears out the ad but doesn't order the book because it's much more expensive than most business books. And even though he or she has the purchase authority to buy it, the executive feels that the price variation is a risk and wants to research the book to see if it's worth the price.

In the first example, the executive buys the luxury car. Even though the price is high, the sales cycle is short because the purchase decision is uncomplicated. In the second example, the price of the equipment is moderate for a corporation, but the sales cycle is long because of the complicated decision process involved. And in the last example of the high-priced book, the sales cycle is longer because of the perception that the risk is high.

Each product and target must be analyzed carefully to determine the appropriate sales cycle and the price/risk relationship. Only then can we determine what is the best way to target individuals precisely where they are in the sales cycle. This is a crucial part of convergence and one of our most valuable strategic tools.

Understand Where the Individual Is in the Sales Cycle

In order to start the relationship, we need to understand the answers to a few crucial questions. Where is the individual in the sales cycle? Are we trying to obtain a sale, a trial, or a lead? Or, are we trying to build brand awareness? And what channels are we going to use?

Once we understand the answers to those questions, we can start moving down the path, strategically. We consider the product or service and the target that we want to sell to. Our job is to bring these two together as cost-efficiently as possible, which means we need to know if the product is high-priced, new, an impulse buy, a complex product, a generic, or a commodity. We need to know if we are going to sell it retail, wholesale, or mail order. Is it consumer or B-to-B? Are we going for repeat sales, or is it a one-shot deal?

As for our target, are there gender or age factors? Is there an education or sophistication factor? What about the demographics? And are there purchase influencers or decision makers in addition to the target? How easy is it to identify the prospect from the general population? And what are the major objections to buying? What is the best media to use to communicate with this individual?

Once we understand the answers to all of these questions, we will have a clear picture of the target individual, a complete understanding of the product, and a much better profile of the individual that this product is designed for, or how and where the product and the target connect.

Getting the Real Answers

Asking the questions is easy. The real challenge is uncovering all of the correct answers to the questions. Over time, I've learned that there are answers to questions and then there are *real answers* to questions. Depending on who you asked in a corporation, you could get very different answers. Your best bet is to get the answers from the folks on the front lines. Then, to get the full picture, gather it all to craft your message. The information regarding the objections to purchase is very important for the copywriter of the ad.

Once we've gathered all of the information, we're ready to form our correct strategy. Sometimes this is easy, and sometimes it is complicated. If you have a new brand of toothpaste entering a commodity product category, I'd want to put more emphasis on the initial branding. We would work on creating a clear differentiation between our new toothpaste and all the other brands, then select the right media to best reach our target. Sales promotions, coupons, free trials, and distribution channel strategies would be used when appropriate. Pinpointing where the new toothpaste company wanted to be on the Rosen Velocity Scale is crucial, as all creative strategy would flow from it.

In the case of a more complex and expensive product, such as a $100,000 network operating system, the business target isn't going to call and order it the first time they see an ad. We know that this is a much longer sales cycle and requires information to ease the target into a comfort level where we can build a long-term relationship.

Conversion Ratios and Sales Flow

Advertising is expensive. It takes a lot of money to create it and more money to place it in a variety of media. So it's critical that it is created, produced, and placed as cost-effectively as possible. This means making accurate projections of the expected interaction and response from the media being used. Also, you must accurately factor in the various conversion ratios at different steps in the sale process. We use Figure 5.2 to help determine how much the client should budget to achieve a particular objective. Think of this as a check and balance tool for your marketing and adverting programs. Use it to figure out what you need the communication to do to move the prospect forward methodically without overstepping any boundaries.

Figure 5.2 Sale Process Flow Chart

Brand-Interaction Worksheet, Revised Budget Allocation

Medium	Typical Interaction Rate	Cost per Interaction	Velocity	Budget per Medium	Interactions per Medium
Brand Print Ads	0.05% to 0.1%	$600	1 – 3		
Brand-Interaction Print Ads	0.3% to 0.75%	$50 – $125	4 – 6		
Inserts	0.05%	$100 – $125	6 – 7		
Direct Mail	.25 to 2.0%	$75 – $200	2 – 4		
Brand-Interaction Direct Mail	1% to 7%	$20 – $100	5 – 7		
DRTV spot (not cable)	n/a	$40	7		
National Brand TV	n/a	$1,000	1		
Radio	n/a	$70 – $250	3 – 7		
Email Marketing	3% to 5%	$60 – $80	4 – 6		
Banner Advertising: Click thru	0.03% to 0.05%	$50 – $70	5		
Tradeshows	n/a	$100 – $200	7 – 10		
Paid Search		$1 – $10	5		
Organic Search		$1 – $10	5		
TOTAL					4800

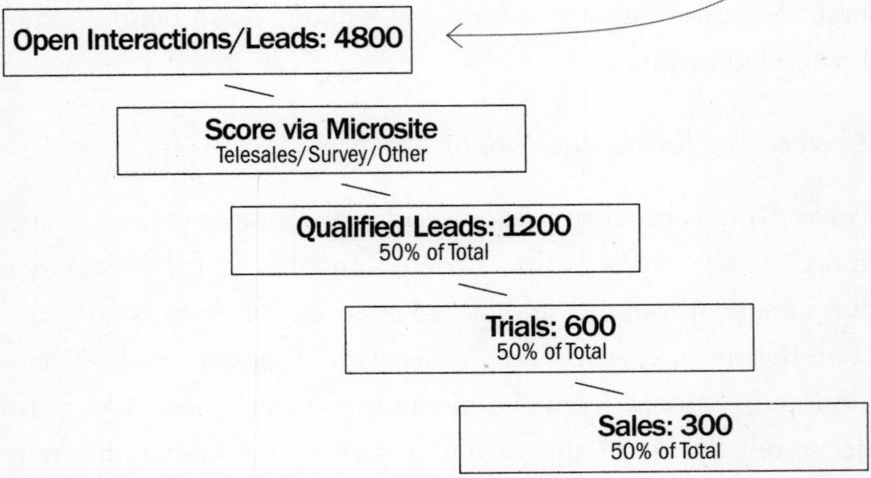

Open Interactions/Leads: 4800

Score via Microsite
Telesales/Survey/Other

Qualified Leads: 1200
50% of Total

Trials: 600
50% of Total

Sales: 300
50% of Total

The way to use this chart is to start from the bottom and work backward.

In this example, our goal is to sell 300 network operating systems at an average price of $50,000, generating gross sales of $15 million. The company is not well known, the product is just being released, it's costly and complex, so it's obvious that you'll need to drive interaction with the brand. The product has to be properly positioned. Its unique features and benefits have to be communicated. Looking at the flow chart, we have some options to explore. It's unrealistic to expect a target to see one ad and order the system, but it is logical to expect the target to be enticed to desire more information. Therefore, our strategy is two-pronged. We need to position the brand and generate interaction in the form of soft (B) and hard (A) leads or BIPs.

So working backward from the 300 sales, we have to get 600 trials because the sales force has a historical closing ratio of 50 percent of individuals who take the trial. From this we know we need 1,200 qualifying leads because the company historically moves 50 percent of qualified leads to trial. This means we need to get 4,800 initial leads. The sales team knows that approximately 25 percent of their open leads will become qualified leads. So how do we get 4,800 open leads? Which media is most cost-effective to reach the target? And how much media do we need to reach the goal of 4,800 leads?

For the sake of simplicity, I'm going to use print. A traditional awareness campaign would pull about a .1 percent response. Using convergence, we can easily increase that to .3 percent. By investing in a brilliant offer, such as a leading edge white paper from an objective third party that resonates with this technology group, we could increase it to maybe a .8 percent response rate. The design of the communication to stimulate interactions has proven to deliver amazing rewards.

To get the 4,800 open leads at an .8 percent rate, we need to buy enough media to get our ads in front of 600,000 target individuals. Think of it as 600,000 views. So in this case, the equation would deliver 600,000 impressions $\times$ .008 $=$ 4,800 interactions.

The media would cost $430,000, with $20,000 of that going toward the rights of the white paper. Plus or minus $50,000 to develop three print ads, our total cost is $500,000 (see Figure 5.3).

The difference in results is staggering. Under the traditional approach, a V1 to V3 ad will receive about .1 percent delivering approximately $2,000,000 in sales. Using convergence at a V4 to V6, we delivered a whopping $15,000,000 with the same budget. How do we do it? We first considered what was needed to accomplish as a short-term benchmark. This unto itself was important. Then we knew how to redesign the low velocity ads to deliver everything the traditional brand ad delivers, plus interaction. If you can build an ad that delivers brand resonance and delivers interaction with the same budget, you are way ahead of the game in today's business environment. Anything else is old stuff, like driving around in a Model T. It looks cool, but it can't

Figure 5.3   Ad Campaign with Budget of $500,000, Comparing Traditional to Convergence

Description	Traditional Approach	Convergence Approach
Total Development of 3 ads	$50,000	$50,000
High-Interest Whitepaper	20,000	20,000
Media Buy	430,000	430,000
Total Cost to reach 600,000 individuals	$500,000	$500,000
Interaction Rate	.1%	0.80%
Open Interaction/Leads	600	4,800
Qualified Interactions/leads (25%)	150	1,200
Trials (50% of qualified Interactions/Leads)	75	600
Sales (50% of trials)	38	300
Gross Sales ($50,000 each system)	$1,900,000	$15,000,000
Note: Example does not include cost to qualifying, fulfillment, trial and field staff		

deliver velocity. Unfortunately, old creative directors die hard, and most are still trying to make that old model work.

TRY THIS AT HOME

To truly grasp how the convergence ad works, I'd like you to try this experiment. Pick up a magazine, one of your favorites, and turn the pages, skimming through it. Your eyes land briefly on each ad. Those that interest you slow you down a bit, as your eyes skim the ad looking for a quick synopsis of the featured product. If you are skimming a traditional ad, your eyes will flow past the call to action because it's buried in the copy that you don't have time to read. Only those with the time and inclination to read all of the copy will spot it.

However, in the case of convergence, the ad is designed for the person who is skimming. Subheads break up the copy into more digestible chunks and pull you into the copy. The call to action is prominent, and depending on the velocity that was strategically selected for the ad, there might even be an enticing limited-time offer to tempt a faster interaction. Based upon these key differences, and the balance of the copy, image, and offer, the convergence ad will pull far more BIPs than a traditional ad. In the preceding example, we projected a .8 percent response versus a .1 percent response. The key difference is that convergence initially generated more interactions and or leads—and as any good salesperson knows, the more qualified interactions/leads you have, the more conversations you will have and sales you'll generate.

For simplicity's sake in the preceding example, we are showing that all the subsequent conversion rates are identical, when in real life, convergence pulls much higher conversion rates at virtually all steps in the sales process. This is due to the follow-up. Face it, most of the follow-up in traditional advertising is mediocre at best. You might get an information sheet that arrives with a boring, impersonal letter. They might even send it in a pretty, overdesigned folder. But do you feel loved? To make matters worse, when a company uses its internal staff to do the follow-up instead of an outside fulfillment house, the request is ignored and nothing is sent out as often as 50 percent of the time.

With convergence, the targets order a FREE DVD that not only explains the product but also sells them on the key benefits. It is accompanied by print material and a well-written sales letter that move them closer to sales. Just prior to having a professional fulfillment house ship the DVD, e-mails or telesales contacts and qualifies them with a few simple questions. Those that are qualified are later contacted by a salesperson and offered a free trial. Those that accept are monitored during the trial period and closed when possible.

Value the Interaction

This is why we must design the ad to get the lead, the interaction point, and not the sale. This is a vital point that is too often overlooked in advertising. If we just did a traditional "hard sell" approach, it would not be as effective. It would be premature, just like the marriage proposal at the beginning of this chapter. It is vitally important that you do not rush the sales process and skip past the preliminary steps.

From a creative standpoint, I want the emphasis to be on educating the individual, not direct selling. This might mean splitting the creative between positioning the product and promoting the information, not the sale. Price, most likely, would not be mentioned. It's too early in the cycle. It could be a turn off if we haven't communicated the value of the system. And because we can't cram all of the relevant information into the ad, we need to get information to them in a different way.

In this situation we could offer a FREE brochure, or whitepaper with a catchy title, or a DVD, or even something else like an invitation to a FREE seminar. The creative has to convince the individual to order the information, whether through the web, an e-mail, regular mail, phone, or even text these days.

The key is not to rush the sales process. Find out where individuals are in the sales cycle and treat them accordingly, with empathy.

THE SALES CYCLE AND HOW IT DRIVES DIALOGUE STRATEGY

We're going to use Figure 5.4, an image of the sales cycle, to understand two vitally important things that are essential to convergence. We'll determine where the individuals are within the sales cycle based upon their response to us. And, we will know how to communicate with them, based upon where they are in the sales cycle. One feeds off the other. We cannot drive a successful dialogue with an individual if we make assumptions. We must respect them where they are and empathetically communicate with them at that exact place. We cannot ask the person we don't have a relationship with to buy, any more than we can ask a stranger to marry us. And this visual of the cycle clarifies where the individuals are, therefore, what we need to communicate,

Figure 5.4   Sales Cycle and Customer Dialogue Strategy

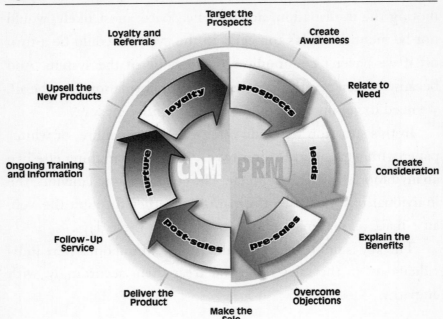

and how we can best dialogue with them. In other words, it allows us to dialogue with the individual no matter where they are in the sales cycle. Using oftentimes the tools of objection selling, gives us a better perspective for developing the empathetic dialogue needed for each segment of the sales process with the individuals.

The image clearly represents the two sides of the sales cycle, before the sale and after the sale. The right side, from noon to six o'clock, represents the individual as a prospect. The left side, from six o'clock to midnight, represents the individual as a customer. So the tools for prospect relationship management work on the right side, and the tools for customer relationship management work on the left. They are entirely separate areas, requiring different tools and must be respected as different. We can never use the wrong tools to build a relationship with the individual.

Targeting the Prospect at Noon

At high noon on the wheel, we are learning. We are using all the tools of research to find out who our targets are and what messaging we need to communicate to them about our products or services. We need to chart it all out. We need to know about the influencers, the decision makers, and the blockers. Refer to the questions I outlined earlier. Trust me, you can never have too much information. This is where your database of marketing information plays a key role in your strategic decision making.

The Awareness Stage at One O'clock

At one o'clock, your messaging is focused on building awareness. You're getting the word out, providing information that will initiate a spark. However, at this stage, you're not going to get a response. Years ago, I was suspect to use offers in this quadrant that had little to do with the brand. Items like Swiss Army knives, flashlights, little tools for engineers, world clocks, and pens that glow will certainly stimulate people. But those who respond are what many of us call suspects, rather than prospects. Suspects are not leads and usually a waste of time and money.

Communications in this first quadrant will not bring us a lot of information about individuals. Our job is to use empathy to make them aware of our product or service and initiate enough stimuli for them to care.

Where the Gold Is: Creating Consideration at Three O'clock

Moving down the wheel, we come to my favorite place, creating consideration. It is the most efficient place for attracting early relationships via all media. At the three o'clock stage, individuals want to interact. Here we can problem solve, ask questions, and create a dialogue that will feed our database. We can cast a wide net and generate the most qualified interactions.

Individuals who respond at this stage will tell you a tremendous amount about themselves. They are actively looking for information and will happily answer questions as long as we provide answers and information that meets their level of interest. However, keep in mind that they are probably having the same dialogue with the competition.

At three o'clock, our strategy is to create consideration points that will inspire individuals to raise their hands. Some of them will spend a lot of time checking us out. Others will make a few quick hits. Either way, we want to talk. Use whatever means they prefer, whether it's the phone, mail, e-mail, or the web. The ultimate is the web because it provides efficiency for the individual. Plus, it makes building that database so much easier.

Once they raise their hands and you start the dialogue, you'll have about half A and B leads, and half C and D leads. The ones who want knowledge in the short term are the A and B leads. About 46 percent will move forward to buy something in this category within 360 days. So the dialogue needs to be empathetic or they might turn to your competition. From 7 percent to 15 percent are your A leads, and from 35 percent to 45 percent are

B leads. These numbers provide the information you need to go to market with reduced business risk. They will help you to strategically craft messaging, offer platforms, and spreadsheets. Based on this initial dialogue, you will move a large percentage of your prospects forward.

Communications designed at three o'clock are optimum for most new customer acquisitions. Not only do you stimulate those that are ready to buy within zero to 90 days, but you also add tremendous leverage when you cast a wider net. If you tie an offer to it, you will increase the number of prospects using the same budget, to include those that will consider and need to buy within 90 to 360 days. A proforma would show that there is gold in them there hills.

Explaining Features and Benefits at Four O'clock

There is a natural break in the dialogue between three o'clock and four o'clock.

From all of the response, you will have a small group who really do want to know more about you. Sending surveys, contacting them with customer service calls, e-mail, and mail are all great media to continue the dialogue. And trust me, you want to take the time; you want to be ready for this level of dialogue because they are closely considering your product.

Moving into Presale at Five O'clock

People who fit into this area of the cycle are definitely having a dialogue with you. They keep returning to your web site. They request different units of information. They want answers to different questions. They need the answers to make an informed decision. You have to keep a sensitive eye on your communications at this point. You don't want to irritate them by sending some prepackaged nonsense that doesn't provide the answers to their questions. You are beyond explaining features and benefits. Each communication is an exchange in which you can, tactfully, move them closer to the sale. You may be sending research, articles, or testimonials. You might even send them information that shows how you fixed a problem. Trust me, this is the true test of a good partner and supplier.

We all judge a company by how they respond to and handle our problems. I learned years ago when running all direct for U.S. Bank that their customers would stay longer than average if we had an opportunity to fix a problem. I have no doubt that the same holds true for others. How we fix those issues makes all the difference, thereby increasing the expected value of the individual. It's how we earn brand loyalty.

At this stage, we are providing information to overcome their objections. It's an ensemble of players as marketing compliments the needs of sales. Integrity is the key, and everyone is on their best behavior because if customers get spooked, or you do not come off as expected, they will be long gone.

Make the Sale at Six O'clock

Time has passed. Some have been in your pipeline for only 30 days, and others have been in dialogue for nearly a year. You have lots of information from all of them to analyze. You made money on those that were easy, and you made more money on those that required nurturing along the way.

Delivering the Goods at Seven O'clock

The old adage, promise what you will and deliver more, is important in today's world. It's time to deliver the product or services and a good time to ask yourself what you've done to wow your customers. What surprised them about you? What unexpected gesture set in motion their positive experience? What made them trust you enough to talk with you as a close friend or colleague?

Follow-Up at Eight O'clock

The next 90 days are critical. Now that customers have the new product or service, their level of satisfaction is critical path. It sets the tone and defines the leverage for all future products they will buy from us. Oh sure, there is a honeymoon period, but I think we all would agree that time is getting shorter by the minute.

From the depths of consumer behavior, most customers go through a period called *postcognitive dissonance*. It is a period after the sale, when we have the new stuff and measure it against ads, competitive products, and preconceived notions, just to reassure ourselves that we made the right decision.

Knowing this, what are you doing to assist your customers, as well as the influencers and decision makers, that they have made the right choice? What you do and how much you can spend on this directly correlates to the size of the sale, but I trust you get the point.

Some companies really work this. They make us feel loved. American Express extends my warranty period and provides a safe harbor. I like that.

Then there are the network printer folks. They come in, give two hours of training to 10 employees, and that's it. The trained employees end up using the 3 features out of 20 that they remember from the training, and none are the wiser. I mean that, literally.

The same issue holds for software. The program is installed, and if you click "help," it will take you through a tutorial. We end up using the few items that relate to our job and then wonder why we spent so much money on it. Not feeling the love.

Nurturing: Show Me the Love at Nine O'clock

One of the best ways to show buyers we care, and nurture the relationship and build brand loyalty, is through the ongoing training and information as it relates to our product. We need to train well and then retrain. Otherwise, the new upgrade or cross-sell comes out, and the very people who should buy it have no idea why they should want it. Because they're only using about half of what the software can do now, they don't know why they need additional features. To make matters even worse, new software comes out by the competition. Because people are not locked into the old software, what the heck, they'll give it a go. Maybe it will be easier to use.

This scenario happens more often than anyone would like to admit. The only way to stop the madness is by nurturing the existing customers. Respect the customers and understand their expected value over some given period of time. They are so much more than a transaction. We all know how hard it is to get new customers, and we need to nurture the ones we have. So stop giving lip service to this age-old problem and take a long hard look at what each of the customers really costs to acquire and what it costs to keep them growing.

Loyalty and Referrals at Ten O'clock

If there was gold in some hills, then there are diamonds in these. Referrals deliver inexpensive sales, period. They do so in days instead of weeks or months, and they are usually at good margin. There is no question in my mind that this is the be all and end all of doing everything almost entirely right.

To better understand the importance of this issue, I highly recommend Fred Reichheld's book *The Ultimate Question: Driving Good Profits and True Growth*. In it, he boils it all down to the net promoter score (NPS), and the bottom line is, would you recommend me to a colleague or friend? It's an excellent read on this subject. It will change the way you go to market around this all-important variable of business.

GOING FULL CIRCLE

The plan is to continue going around this circle with each of the individuals you meet. You bring them in, earn their trust, and build a relationship with them, as well as with all of their family and friends. Each message is empathetic, reaching out to them with care, allowing give and take within the direction of the dialogue. It's how we create brand resonance, through dialogue.

The purpose of this tool is to help you understand exactly where the targets are, based upon how they react or communicate with you. Take the time to understand, analyze, and evaluate how each section of the sales cycle and customer dialogue relates you to your business. It will enhance your dialogue with your team and, again, work to bring the silos of marketing, sales, IT, and finance together, and understand what you all need to do in order to achieve your shared goal.

6

The Ask and the Offer

Let me begin by asking the $64 million question: *What are you asking individuals to do when they see your advertisement?* You must want them to do something, so why not use that beautiful image to drive them to interact? Let's look at a few critical variables with better-defined *ask* to drive our marketing and advertising programs like they're on steroids.

More Meaningful Headlines

Meaningful headlines go a long way to stimulate the individual to get involved with your brand. Some use the double entendre, or a play on words. These can be creative, yet void of meaning. Don't fall into that trap. We're not using art for art's sake. Use strong, emotional headlines that hit the prospect in the heart, not the head. Choose powerful words that do more than grab attention—they drive meaning. You don't need to sacrifice creative because you want to stand out of the clutter, but keep it believable. The purpose is to pull the individual in and move them quickly to interaction. Here are a few examples:

Company: i-Opener
Headline: *All the Fun of the Internet, without a Computer*
Product: First home Internet appliance with instant on and web access

Company: Neodata (EDS)
Headline: *Find and Keep Customers by Building Relationships*
Product: B-2-B database provider to help electric utilities facilitate market share capture

Company: Pacific Power and Light
Headline: *Dry Rot Mildew Mold . . . A Homeowner's Nightmare! Only now there's a logical low-cost solution*
Product: Utility provider to second home owners of coastal property who aren't there much during winter

Company: Pacific Power and Light
Headline: *Don't Put Up with Another Hot, Sticky, Sweltering Summer . . . Read on to Beat the Heat*
Product: Utility provider stimulating heat pump sales

Company: Rand McNally
Headline: *Don't Plan This Year's Vacation with Last Year's Information*
Product: Retail and web-based maps, for the DVD upgrade to a software program

Company: Tektronixs (Xerox)
Headline: *WANTED: For Killing a Great Idea with a Boring Presentation*
Product: Major provider of color network printers

Company: Merant
Headline: *It's just a few website changes . . . can I have them today. . . . PLEASE?!!*
Product: Major provider of web content software

Company: Lucent
Headline: *Find the weak links in your enterprise before someone else does*
Product: Major telecommunications provider of network solutions

Company: Lightscape
Headline: *THIS IS NOT A PHOTOGRAPH. IT'S YOUR COMPETITIVE EDGE.*
Product: Software for architectural, 3-D rendering applications

Company: Gemstone Systems
Headline: *Don't trust your Enterprise JavaBeans to any new kid on the block*
Product: Enterprise software pioneer, adoption of enterprise infrastructure

BEHAVIORAL CHANGE AGENTS: THE OFFER

Adding behavioral change agents to stimulate interaction is another magic bullet. I don't care how brilliant the advertising seems, there's always room for a reason to move forward, and it will enhance your brand. Don't let your creative director tell you otherwise. Behavioral change agents can take on many forms. I highly recommend topical *offers* that compliment the brand-to-build resonance, such as the following examples:

- A whitepaper that is meaningful and nonbiased
- A glove-compartment-size safety guide if you're selling cars
- A DVD that is entertaining and informative
- A book or design portfolio
- A socially responsible microsite for a cause you are sponsoring
- A financial tool to analyze retirement, investments, and savings
- Countless others

The offer is, without a doubt, one of the most powerful variables. I think it's possible to sell just about anything if I use a really great offer. It can certainly rescue even the worst idea and reinforce the foundation of the brand. It makes the ad exciting. For the offer to succeed, we must present it with honesty and integrity to win the respect of today's sophisticated customer.

A Major Driver to Move Individuals Forward

Direct marketers have always used offers to move the individual forward in the sales process. They would test and retest offer A versus offer B against a battery of test cells to find which one gave the biggest bang for the buck. Testing used to be the core of good direct marketers, but it has drastically reduced in the operating environments of the last 10 years. But in its heyday, the direct marketing group tested everything. They learned that just because a thing works the first time, it doesn't mean it will work the second or third time. To settle for repeating variables that worked in the past, near or distant, is a strategy doomed for failure. Any firm that embraces testing, especially testing offers, is a winner in the long term.

Change Is the Only Constant

The ever-changing offer can make things interesting and exciting. It's usually the difference between ultimate success and failure and the most critical variable if you want to build brand while generating interaction faster, with less budget, and with far better ROI over time.

Actualizing and Substantiating Your Brand

The list of topical offers to compliment your brand is endless. Take a pragmatic look at offers you can use throughout the campaign that help define what your brand stands for and help define the business you are in:

- Are you in the oil business or the energy business?
- Are you in the auto or transportation business?
- Are you in the business of selling windows or beautifying the home?
- Are you selling stone pavers for patios and driveways, or are you in the business of beautifying of the exterior environments of the home?

These nurturing techniques are never to be used to close the sale. That approach will send your e-mail, mail, or telephone call into the trash bin. You need to raise the bar and deliver value to your prospects and customers beyond the sale. Be proactive. Show us what your brand stands for, and give your target something useful, earning the respect and trust you need to make the sale while building a long-term relationship.

The bottom line is that the headline and offer must be honest, credible, and about the individual. The overall communication needs to dance down the page. Think of yourself as skiing or kayaking. The copy needs to flow like the rhythm of your hips. You don't need to tell us everything, just enough to move us forward.

What about Accountability?

Accountability begins with performance. The ad must perform. A tight headline, the right copy, a gripping image, and a great ask and offer with a velocity of V4 and up will give you a hardworking ad that delivers interaction.

If you use a call to action, design it to go to one or several tuned microsites, rather than the main web site. The microsite should be designed to immediately engage them into a dialogue and have the same look and feel of the creative ad with the call to action, so they recognize it and feel comfortable. But don't lead them to the corporate web site and force them to search through the mission statement, press releases, products, and services, leading them further and further into the depths of hell in search of the offer. You will lose them. They will neither like you nor trust you after that adventure. Send them to a microsite where they will recognize the same look as the advertisement and easily spot the respective meaningful offer on the unique landing page. You will gain meaningful interaction, plus the ability to measure the activity and earn real-time accountability, and a new level of performance for the program.

Martha, Get My Glasses

The web address should be larger than eight-point type, or it won't drive traffic. Remember, our job is to sell stuff and make money for our client, and you may need to remind your art director of that fact. Balance the ad for the media with the things that will drive the individual to the brand.

TRANSFORMING THOUGHT

Now you're ready to move forward and use different media to build brand resonance. The old borders of above- and below-the-line communications are intertwined in mission. We have the technology, the art, and the science to deliver far more interactions, building resonance faster with less money than before. Some use a tight call to action as the first step in the sales process, and others use a more open approach. Both have their place.

Turning the "Valve" Up and Down as Needed

We all understand why we want to increase interaction, but sometimes we need to decrease interactions. Keep in mind that we want to obtain quality leads, especially when we factor in the cost of time required to convert the interaction into a sale. The quantity must be weighted against the quality. Our task is to deliver qualified interactions to the sales force at the precise moment they need them. Realizing the difficulty of this task, we need to establish an understanding with the VP of sales about the balance of quantity and quality.

Let's say the sales force already has ample leads to work on, and they don't have time to qualify huge stacks of new leads. Using the metaphor of a valve that we tighten or loosen to control the flow of leads, we would tighten the valve at this point so only the highly qualified would get through. By testing, we can determine precisely how tight we need to turn the valve.

However, other instances, such as a company with a large sales force starving for leads, might want the valve turned to wide open. Obviously, every sales person wants good, solid, qualified interactions. However, in this case, a weaker or less qualified interaction is better than none at all.

Predetermine the Criteria with Sales

In the previous chapter on the sales cycle and customer dialogue, I showed how interactions are classified into A through D leads. Classifying the interactions sets the expectation with the sales team. My advice is to work with the sales team to predetermine the criteria for each level of A through D leads. In my experience, this level of communication is an important variable to a respectful relationship between marketing, advertising, and sales. You have to take and share ownership and make sure you're all speaking the same language.

Table 6.1   Purchase Time Frame for Different Interactions/Leads

A	B	C	D
A = 0–30 days	B = 30–90 days	C = over 90 days	D = never
A = 0–90 days	B = 90–180 days	C = over 180 days	D = never
A = 1–3 months	B = 3–6 months	C = over 6 months	D = never
A = 1–6 months	B = 6–18 months	C = over 18 months	D = never

The purchase time frame for the different leads can vary dramatically at each company (see Table 6.1). More complex, expensive products usually take longer simply because more people are involved in the decision-making process. Selling an expensive product to a government agency that requires special approvals and appropriations can run into years. The main point is to pick a time line that is based on historical sales information.

Controlling Your Results

Most people in marketing and advertising view lead generation as a hit-and-miss situation. You launch a promotion and pray it will generate the number of quality interactions you're in search of to placate the voracious appetite of the sales force. But you can gain control over your interactions and tailor them exactly to the needs of your company by combining the valve metaphor with the Velocity Scale.

The Math of the Tight Valve Approach

In the following tight valve example (Table 6.2), you can see that the better the interaction, the higher the conversion rate. More are ready to buy and require less effort.

Table 6.2   Tight Valve Approach: 1,200 Interactions

Quality	Number	Conversions	Appointments	Orders	Total $$
	#			30%	
A(20%)	300	50%	150	45	900,000
B(40%)	600	25%	150	45	900,000
C(20%)	300	10%	30	9	180,000
Total	1,200		330	99	$1,980,000

The chart includes total interactions from brand-interaction vehicles including V5 print ad, V6 mail, V3 e-mail, and V4 television spot, to brand and sell a product with an average price of $20,000 at various interaction rates. The program cost totals $250,000. You generated 1,200 interactions.

In the following loose valve approach (Table 6.3), we now acquired 4,000 interactions and increased the number of leads in all categories. The downside is that the number of C and D leads skyrocketed. The upside is that we picked up more A and B leads, generating additional millions in sales. Note that we have not taken into account the increase in fulfillment, but in this business case, with such a high unit of sale, the proforma will be positive.

Table 6.3   Loose Valve Approach: 4,000 Interactions

Quality	Number	Conversions	Appointments	Orders	Total $$
	#		50%	30%	
A(20%)	800	50%	400	120	2,400,000
B(40%)	1,600	25%	400	120	2,400,000
C(20%)	800	10%	80	24	480,000
D(20%)	800		0	0	
Total	4,000		880	264	$5,280,000

In this type of business, factor in $5 to $20 for interaction capture and fulfillment, and maybe $10 to $20 per individual starting off, to nurture the B and C leads as appropriate throughout the year.

Techniques to Tighten or Loosen the Valve

With today's technology, we don't need to give sales bad leads. There are plenty of centralized screening processes and other off-the-shelf nurturing programs that reside within your best fulfillment houses. If you find you're giving low quality leads to your sales team, stop. The human cost is far too great to waste time on cold or non-nurtured leads. Do your research. Check out the Sales Leads Management Association at www.saleslead mgmtassn.com. You need to put the right program in place, and you might need to tweak the ad to better pull the quality of leads you want to deliver.

PRACTICAL APPLICATIONS

In the spring of 2008, I had the pleasure of consulting with the CEO of System Pavers out of Orange County, California. They are in the business of making our homes more beautiful by selling and installing paving stones for your driveway, patio, and walkways. It's a wonderful concept that adds texture while increasing home value and curb appeal.

Like many companies, System Pavers focused their advertising by selling the concept of how beautiful your home would look with pavers. The call to action was for the customer to request a consult with a salesperson to come to your home. Once there, the salesperson would show you an image of your present home and then how an image of your home with the enhancement of their product. To put this into perspective, the ask in this case is at five o'clock on the customer sales cycle and dialogue chart (Figure 5.4).

System Pavers is not unique in their approach when it comes to the ask.

Other manufacturers and resellers such as Anderson Windows, Pella, most electric and gas home heating and air conditioning (HVAC) folks and many on the B-to-B side use this level of ask, from all sorts of media. Some use problem solution, some use short copy, and some use long copy. What they all have in common is tying the ask to the last part of the sales process, right before the close. But how many of us want a salesperson at the door trying to close us? Even if we're late in the sales cycle and have pain, we may not want a salesperson in our home or place of business as the first interaction with the firm. This approach can scare off lots of folks before you ever get a chance to talk with them. At the bottom line, it appears there's nothing wrong because they all make money and have been in business for years. But they could greatly increase performance by simply changing the ask. Right now, they are focused on the A leads only, a mere 10 percent of all possible inter-actions. Changing the ask to a loose approach, at three o'clock in the dialogue, maybe the ticket to make even more.

System Pavers Makes the Transition

Systems Pavers and I embarked on such a mission. Via brand-interaction TV spots, mail, radio, and print, with all communications designed at V4 to V7 on the scale, we launched a pilot.

Keeping all controls in place to give statistical validity without causing any disruption to the current business, we isolated key markets to understand our results with utmost precision. A few of the many creative executions follow, testing the ask at three o'clock and five o'clock, both separately and together.

Figure 6.1 shows a self-mailer vehicle as the new format, highlighting the beauty of the products with a more visual approach. The ask is at five o'clock with a V7 in velocity.

In addition to testing the control with the ask at five o'clock, we proceeded to test two highly successful offers at three o'clock and five o'clock.

Figure 6.2 shows the ask at two levels. The first represents what I call a *topical/topical offer*. In this case, we used a DVD kit and a beautiful book of design projects for the outside living area of your home. One is at five o'clock and the second is at three o'clock. Note the short but critical screening questions for the nurturing of all B and C leads.

We also tested a second self-mailer, not shown, using a topical/nontopical offer, directed at the customer at three o'clock and five o'clock in the dialogue. We used the Free DVD Kit along with the non-topical two pints of Häagen-Dazs ice cream. The ice cream gift certificates are fulfilled at your local grocery store. This offer has proven to be my best performer in the non-topical category to compliment a topical offer. I've never used the ice cream or any non-topical offer by itself. Brand integrity is too important.

Brand-interaction print at V6 was used to stimulate interaction across an array of verticals (see Figure 6.3). In this test case, the ask at three o'clock is going for a wide net, or loose valve,

Figure 6.1   System Pavers Self-Mailer Vehicle, 20% Off, V7, Five O' Clock

Figure 6.2 System Pavers, Self-Mailer Vehicle, SC, Letter/DVD/Book, V7, Three O' Clock and Five O' Clock

Figure 6.3   System Pavers Print with DVD/Book Offer, V6, Three O' Clock

approach. The DVD and design book together were our strongest set of offers, although expensive and heavy to fulfill. I recommend that you start with your best and test downward to find your optimum cost/interaction/sales ratios.

There were many ways for the individual to interact, including microsites. In Figure 6.4, microsites are personalized where appropriate. These were designed specifically for each audience and promotion. Brand-interaction TV was also used as fuel for real-time investment, driving individuals to interaction with

Figure 6.4   Microsites, V4

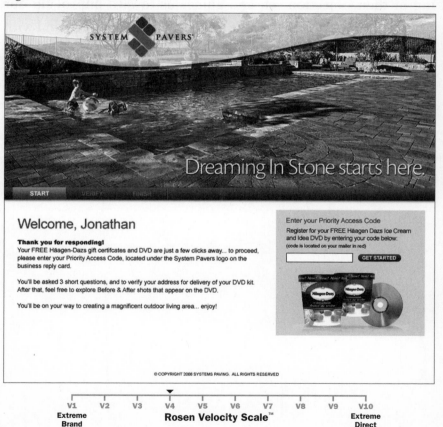

topical offers at three o'clock and five o'clock. The point of action at three o'clock was to spark interaction with an offer, and at five o'clock we asked for an appointment to close.

To conclude, the results of this dynamic pilot are confidential, but I can assure you they were *very* positive! The challenge is to test the expanded options on the table.

The ask is more efficient when it's tied to *proof of concept* and *true interest*. Expanding the scope of interaction will have tremendous gains for the growth of the company. It expands our knowledge of customers and prospects, deepens our understanding of their objection set, and guides us toward improving our marketing and advertising. We can build brand and demand with the same budget faster. Building brand resonance and demand are now one.

The next step is learning how to leverage real-time accounting to earn the support and respect of your CFO.

7

EXPECTED VALUE OF THE INDIVIDUAL

Know these few numbers . . . and you too will make you and your firm a fortune.

Convergence uses simple math to accurately determine the value of a customer. One of the most important variables is the contribution margin to profit. In short, it is how much money you will make after selling something today plus the up-sell or cross-sell over some time period later.

After we take away direct variable cost associated with the initial and follow-up sales, you are left with a most powerful number that tells what the individual is worth now and over time, to drive the convergence marketing machine.

The simple formula is:

Contribution Margin (CM) = Total sales less Cost of Goods Sold (COGS)

I'll walk you through this simple example. A product sells for $1,000. A normal cost of goods sold (COGS) might be 40 percent or $400 *direct variable* expense. If you were to take this sum, subtract it from $1,000 actual dollars received, you have $600 from the up-front transaction.

Action	Initial Sale	COGS	CM
Sale	1,000	40%	600

Now suppose that for every $1,000 sale, you could count on each customer purchasing accessories worth $200, at a fixed price that has a COGS of 60 percent Simple math tells us that this would give you additional profits of $80 (60% x $200).

In total, you would have gross sales of $1,200. You had various COGS, but in the end, you netted $600 + $80, for a total of $680 CM for each sale made. In this example, you received all your money at once, as illustrated in the following.

Action	Initial Sale	Accessories	Total	COGS-1	CM-1	COGS-2	CM-2	Total CM
Add-On	1,000	200	1,200	<400>	600	<120>	80	680

Cost of Capital

Assume you received the cash for selling those accessories or add-ons in year two. You would then discount those moneys by what is called the *cost of capital*. Over the years, 7 to 10 percent seems to be acceptable. You'll want to work with your finance person to establish the percentage they believe the cash is costing them. In this example, I simply discounted the CM of what would have been $80 by 10 percent or $8, and it is now netting you $72 for those accessory sales made one year from the date of the original sale, as illustrated in the following example. Needless to say, with more zeros attached, it adds up fast and gets a lot more interesting and important.

Action	Initial Sale	Accessories	Total	COGS-1	CM-1	COGS-2	CM-2	COC	Total CM
Add-On	1,000	200	1,200	<400>	600	<120>	80	<8>	672

Getting your financial team involved early will go a long way toward making all the corporate influencers, blockers, and decision makers allies throughout the entire program cycle.

Discounting for Risk of Time

Another important variable is discounting for risk of time. You know that some of the customers to whom you sold the $1,000 item will buy accessories. You just don't know for certain how many will buy a year from now. You were willing to take the CM on the accessories if the additional sale happened at the same time; however, one year from now is an entirely different story. You discounted for cost of capital; however, you now need to discount further. This is considered additional business risk and must be included in your equation for future earnings. Having this accurate portrayal of financial facts will build confidence in your business case.

To accurately understand what a sale is worth today, when it isn't sold until the following year, requires reliable data to make a low-risk determination. This issue has stopped many a marketing and finance person and ended in impasse. Short of going into full net present value computations, I have taken a very pragmatic view and found a good low risk solution for all.

Start with the right information. You must have a database that has the information you need in one place. Start with the research folks; they know where everything is and are the brain trust of the company. For starters, look at sales from last year and track which customers bought what and when they bought it. Go back three to five years and look at those numbers as well. Write a notes section of what variables made up the situations for those years. Throw out anomalies that you cannot rely on happening again. Things like a huge product launch with outrageous PR that flooded the market, or a natural disaster, or your competition launched a new product in the same space. Look at those wonderful or not so wonderful items and write them down. What are your coefficients to sales? What are you explanatory variables that shape what your customers will buy from you next? Think of the variables as dials to tune up or tune down. I call them *positive reenforcers* and *negative reenforcers*. List each under its respective heading. With this analysis in hand, you're almost ready.

Of all customers buying one year from now, 100 percent will be worth $672. This represents $600 CM for the first sale and $8.00 in discount (10 percent cost of capital, [COC] on the additional $80 earned for selling accessories one year out). But wait! How many of them will give you the extra $72 one year from now? You know that in years past, 70 percent of all customers bought accessories. Digging further, you found 30 percent attrition (i.e. those that are gone) broken down as follows:

- 7 percent went out of business.
- 10 percent didn't need the accessories.
- 3 percent didn't really like your product and stopped using it.
- 10 percent had a change of labor that weren't trained to use it.

What else would change this equation, and how confident are you in your analysis?

Common Sense Test

You have your research, and you've looked at all of the issues and numbers that make up your expected sales into the future. Let's put it in perspective.

Is it reasonable to assume, with all of these negative and positive reenforcers outlined, that from this $1,000 sale today, you will generate sales of $200 on accessories one year out to 70 percent of these customers?

Only you can answer this, but for my money, it seems reasonable. If the answer is yes, then the expected value of the customer one year out from an initial sale made today will be calculated as follows:

Simply take the $72 that was discounted CM of $80 at 10 percent cost of capital.

Multiply $72 by 70 percent. This gives you $50.40 in accessory CM one year out.

The net present value (NPV) one year out with 30 percent attrition gives you a discounted CM on accessories of $50. To sum up, you made $600 on the original sale. We can now accurately determine that a sale made one year later by adding $50 in CM to each. Taking all this into account, you have a new expected value of $650, rather than the previous guesstimates of $600 or $680. This is a more accurate number that should be reflected on your pro-forma. Your CFO is now very happy. Imagine how important this becomes when adding many more zeros.

It's important to note that you will never know exactly what one individual or business is worth overtime. However, you can rely on the statistics of a group to make accurate calculations of what they're worth. Statistics are part of your rationale, and there are folks around to assist. I find that the research folks generally enjoy the dynamics of the discussion.

Why Working with Finance Changes Everything

I had the pleasure to work with Disney's Magic Kingdom Club (MKC) for a number of years. We were charged with increasing membership. Their past promotions had consisted of print advertising and a professional looking #10 business envelope addressed to human resource (HR) directors. Unfortunately, this program received a low response rate in mail and nothing in print. So I needed to understand what was really going on behind the scenes, and here's what I discovered:

- The human resource departments said the MKC club used 20 percent or more of the HR person's time. In essence, he or she became a travel director for all of the employees who want the MKC discount card to the parks. In short, the HR departments didn't want to deal with it—understandably.
- Worse yet, this same HR person becomes a de facto expert, providing information to all the interested employees on what MKC has to offer, on top of their HR responsibilities.

Mickey, we have a problem! Human resource directors never respond, probably adding the mail to their recycle bin. The MKC is scary stuff. The MKC budget was fine for what eventually became a disposable campaign. But we needed a new strategy. So we came up with an engaging 3-D package that would kick through the clutter, make it through to the HR director, and interest his or her team. The only problem was we needed 10 times the budget to pull it off—and make them a fortune.

The Big Meeting with the Corporate Financial Officer

I made an overture to present my business case to the CFO of the operating division. Our meeting began with his salvo. He'd read my material but didn't think it mattered because all of these folks come to the park anyway. Great. But I was just getting warm, so I asked him if there was anything else he wanted to dispel about the purpose of the MKC division. I proceeded with the facts:

- There are 4,000 club directors.
- Those companies that have a MKC director stay for a minimum of 7 years, more often exceeding 10 years.

- On average, X employees from those companies to go to one of the parks each year.
- They stay an average of X days and spend Y dollars.
- The MKC crafts the entertainment and restaurants for the members to use while they're there, gaining Z percent more of their wallet share than that of other visitors.

This went on for a while, and I think we were both having a good time. He played devil's advocate and, armed with my numbers, I disputed every item on his list. He was a joy to work with. The bottom line was that when we sold an MKC club to a firm with 500 or more employees, and put in an active MKC director who put up Mickey posters and flyers in the lunchroom, the following assumptions held true:

- The company would be with us for a minimum of five years.
- The company, on the margin, would give Disney over $15,000 in CM.
- Anything more than $1,000 per sale was unacceptable.

We had the CFO's blessing to move forward. The first of many promotions ran, consisting of a large 3-D package delivered to 4,900 HR directors with 500 or more employees. Inside the big UPS shipper was a fun red box. Inside were Mickey ears and a background of fun places in the park. The headline read "Welcome to the Best Employee Benefit Program Ever." Inside a fold was a letter inviting them to join, a brochure, and an order vehicle.

Drum roll please! The package pulled 12 percent to order. Getting past the gatekeeper and the bullpen that makes up the selling environment, everyone in the HR department knew something fun had come from Disney because we all recognize the icon of the ears, and we want our turn to wear them.

Analyzing the Results with the Corporate Financial Officer: Oh, Happy Day

The meeting with the CFO went well, as you might imagine. On his whiteboard, we had a wonderful time analyzing the results, as follows:

- We acquired over 583 companies who said yes.
- The cost per acquired company was $129, well below our $1,000 mark.
- 583 companies x $15,000 minimum CM generated over $8,700,000 in first year CM alone.
- Each company would be with us a minimum of five years, giving us a gross of $75,000 with a NPV summed at $48,000 each.
- 583 sales x $48,000 per company in CM delivered millions.

Do the math! The math will set you free. This program received a Gold Echo, and my client and I were both very proud.

DIFFERENTIAL ACCOUNTING

Any discussion of the math that determines the expected value of the individual would not be complete without the concept of differential accounting. It is also referred to as *marketing on the margin*. How useful it will be for you honestly depends on how you and your CFO view it. You don't want to disagree on this. Marketing and the use of real-time accountable advertising is either seen as successful or not, depending on how these terms are factored into the equations. This is the one area that comes back to haunt most marketing folks, and we all should have paid better attention in those cost accounting classes. Here's a crash course.

Many believe the only legitimate costs when figuring the CM are short-term variable overhead and the direct cost attached to the program. On the other hand, many CFOs and cost accountants believe their job is to make sure every bit of overhead is accounted for, across all units sold. They have to put it somewhere. Accounting and finance will not only figure the direct and proper variable COGS, but will also burden these COGS with erroneous overhead assumptions on each unit sold. Existing sales units going out the door are usually divided by the entire plant, equipment, and labor costs, right down to recovering what was spent on paper towels in the washroom.

Is the product your about to sell on the margin? In other words, is the overhead going to stay constant regardless of whether you sell nothing or 100,000 units? Or will it change? This very key issue, if not uncovered early, will cause a company to act far too conservatively. They will think of marketing and advertising expenditures as risky business. It's unfortunate—suicidal, actually. In fact, investing in brand and demand is not nearly as risky as doing nothing, or worse, trying to build brand awareness through the legacy model.

A Stimulating Example

A few years ago, I had the pleasure of working with a very smart VP of marketing in the coffee business. I was striving to deliver a low-risk, B-to-B, new customer acquisition plan. The campaign was supposed to deliver great brand awareness, leading to brand resonance, culminating with lead acquisition for the sales force. The sales force would then give presentations to new restaurants or prospects, generating new sales in numbers this firm could only dream of. The VP and I were trying to figure if we spent $250,000, then how many more pounds of coffee representing how many accounts would have to be acquired within 180 days to pay for this level of budget expenditure? It seemed like it should be simple, but it wasn't. For this example, a pound of coffee cost the firm in direct variable expense about $2.50. It sold for $6.00 to distributors. On the surface, we have a great CM of $3.50/pound of coffee sold.

To see how realistic it would be to break even on advertising for this additional promotion, we take our advertising expenditure of $250,000 and divide by $3.50, which in this case was our direct variable CM. The total sales required to break even would be at a little less than 72,000 pounds. It all seemed doable when we considered the number of interactions projected via the web, print, and direct mail, with follow-up via phone. In fact, our break-even was only 50 accounts—and better yet, we were projected to deliver some 150 new accounts within 180 days.

The math looked good to deliver a low-risk, high-reward program. The VP of marketing liked it. I liked it. I was comfortable with three times break-even, as we were looking for a low- to moderate-risk program. The big surprise came when the CFO looked at draft one and informed us that we forgot to include the overhead for each pound of coffee. So, okay, I thought I'd be magnanimous and add 10 percent. But the reality was that the CFO needed another $2.50 for overhead for each pound of coffee. That was his normal rate of overhead for that year and for his low level of factory utilization.

Our job in marketing and advertising is to grow the business. Using his math, we were burdened with an overhead across the entire business, bringing the total COGS to $5/pound. The disconnect was painfully clear; no new labor or overhead is needed to deliver the inventory to be sold. No new warehouse space is needed. No additional lights need to be turned on for the existing shifts. No additional trucks, nor even staples, pencils, or paper are required.

Marketing is often about working on the margin. In this situation, would you recommend that we spend the $250,000 to accomplish the sales, financial and branding objectives? It's a simple question. The program costs $250,000. The wholesale price is $6, minus the now new-burdened COGS of $5. Sad to say, you are now left with a CM of only $1/pound.

Divide the advertising budget of $250,000 by $1, and you determine that we need to sell 250,000 pounds of coffee just to break even. That's over three times the original sales requirement. It appears the business is not worth pursuing; the risk is far too high. But is it really? Marketing has been stopped cold for fear of the very numbers that, when viewed differently, would have moved the whole agenda of building brand and demand with the same budget positively forward. The program would have been successful. It would have contributed hundreds of thousands of pounds of coffee in the first year alone. Investment spend with low risk would be repeated. Eventually, we would take the warehouse, currently at 50 percent capacity, to something much higher. On the margin, marketing would accomplish its job.

Adding insult to injury, the firm later ran pure branding ads at a V1 for more money, reveling in its old ways by throwing away money with legacy advertising. I'm sure it made them all feel good, despite the fact that I am sure they failed as before to grow the business.

Marketing and finance will work better together in the future than they do today. Imagine a CFO who says, "I want you to make the company money. I need you to do what you do best!" We just have to earn trust with proven results. It's a simple problem made complex by a cultural divide. There are those that believe we must conserve and protect, and others who understand why we need to take calculated risks on the margin, in real time, to achieve unprecedented financial success. Knowing what you can make on the margin is key to every business. Few corporate operational structures encourage and leverage the very wins they want and need. Worse still, after a win, we often have to wait months or a year to go back out and do it again. Waiting is high risk. Leveraging real time knowledge is opportunistic gain.

8

REAL-TIME ACCOUNTING
Numbers That Will Set You Free

Today is always a good day to make profits. Real-time accounting reaches far beyond our current performance measurements because the ad budget will not be based on some percentage of last year's sales, which is the way we've always done it, I know. Please strike that justification from your vocabulary! Real-time accounting uses performance measurements based on the expected value of the new customer over a specific set time. More specifically, we invest in considered budgets, seize the win in the present, and reinvest to continue generating sales by taking calculated risks in known market conditions. Never knowing what one customer will do, we can comfortably rely on the power of the test statistic, which tells us what many will do, based on a confident past. We drive the investment and reinvestment strategies needed to win in our globally competitive markets. When we're able to see the positive results of our spending in both the short and long term, everyone from the C-suite down will want to keep on investing. Real-time accounting lets you drive brand and demand over and over again with consistency—the best way to kill your competition.

WINNING BIG WITH MICHAEL DELL

Michael Dell knew how to use real-time accounting and take calculated risks to win big. I think that's why he was so much fun to work with back in the early 1990s. It was an exciting time, and I was constantly being summoned back to Austin to strategize and create the next revolution of direct response advertising. I remember one day in particular, in a conference room with Michael Dell, John Ellett, and several others, including my pal Janet Rubio, their VP of direct marketing. We were all obsessed with taking the latest profits and investing them right back into the advertising. We developed the strategy and tactics for the upcoming year, and our team efforts helped to make Dell Computer the only firm in history to go from less than one billion in sales to over two billion in one year.

Dell understood the power of accountability. In the early 1990s, as the story goes, Dell would borrow about a half-million per week to run ads in the *Wall Street Journal*. They were brilliant ads that made powerful statements and got customers to pick up the phone and call. The beauty of those ads was that Dell was selling in real time. The A leads would shop and buy right then and there. And we also knew the B leads were worth a fortune. Customers would call, shop, and not buy just yet, but a significant percentage of them would come back and buy later. It was all about seizing the day to keep on investing in real time. Finance and marketing were joined at the hip, and Dell became one of the world's greatest success stories. You could say it was Michael's bold idea to circumvent distributors and go directly to customers that made him successful or that it was the quality of his products and services. And all of that is partly true. But Dell's calculated risk of investment spending based on real-time win was the true magic that propelled his success into the stratosphere—and killed his competition.

One of the Best Compliments of My Career

Fast forward to 2003. I was at DHL's corporate offices in Florida, and I was talking with their director of corporate advertising. My experience at Dell came up. She had worked for Compaq Computer, which was one of Dell's primary competitors, at the same time I was working with Dell. She began to say something, stopped, looked at me as though the lights had just come on, and said, "I get it now. You were at Dell, and this is how you invested the way you did. We were on big but static budgets, and you were on a dynamic path that was unstoppable. You totally outspent us. You were in real time and didn't have to wait three months for awareness and preference scores. You guys killed us." "Yes," I said. "We did."

The Perfect Vehicle for Real-Time Accounting

In a word, the perfect vehicle for real-time accounting is the Internet. Web advertising is the perfect vehicle for real-time everything. It's essentially the performance matrix from the retail roots of marketing and advertising. It offers us the ability to measure and project what is working and what is not—*as it's happening*. This marketing variable is the key to regaining control of spending while increasing the success of our offline programs.

We see it everyday in retail advertising. They use real-time measurement across all of their offline media, and it's the closest thing to the dynamics of the Internet. Offline retail has always delivered, running ads in all shapes and sizes, with calls to action that prompt customers to come down, incenting them with great offers. Retail is all about real-time measurement. However, retailers were about the only folks doing it.

Real-time accountable advertising requires creative that not only builds awareness, but also builds brand resonance faster, using less of the budget. Ads that work best are in the V4 to V6 range on the Velocity Scale. The brand folks get everything they need to build great advertising. The direct folks put it on steroids that look good. Combined in the same vehicle, they have a better advertising product across all media and channels, delivering a stronger relationship with the brand. You have a new way to leverage your existing budget and deliver more with each unit of money spent. Your C-level team will be very happy.

Seeing Is Believing: A Few Examples

Bose Corporation does a brilliant job of balancing the drive to interaction with all of their real-time accountable ads. They know what they're getting for their money in both short- and long-term time frames. It's far beyond the static budget. Selling their low-end CD/Radio directly forms the up-sell and cross-sell path for their true moneymakers, the $2,000 to $6,000 systems sold via retail, catalog, and other channels. Delivered by their use of a robust database engine, their nurturing campaigns keep you coming back. Their ads are well crafted, and each of the key variables, from creative to finance to offer, are a model of convergence. Think about it; they were once a relatively small firm that has built a brilliant brand over time. Like Dell, their commitment to keep on spending with confidence is their strategic weapon.

Tempur-Pedic, the space-age bed folks, and the Sleep Number Bed from Select Comfort are two more examples that use real-time accounting to drive their media machines. And both seem to be successfully taking on the established bed manufacturers. Both rely on real-time budgets and are well positioned on the margin to take market share from their huge competitors.

500 Commercials Later

I attended Cannes Lion in 2007 as a keynote speaker, and one afternoon I must have sat through 500 television commercials, all of which were the quintessential "highly creative" ads being considered for the awards, and all with low velocity of about V1, maybe a V2 here and there. Worse yet, and sad to say, it was difficult to know what a good many of them they were selling. Listen, I am all for great creative. I love brilliant ads with gorgeous creative. I love being wowed as much as the next person. But it's difficult to watch knowing that no matter how brilliant the creative is, this low velocity, this form of advertising, requires tremendous frequency. But the budgets aren't there. Yet they continue to build the same ads with the hopes that creativity will lead them to the Holy Grail.

CONVERGENCE: THE *DA VINCI CODE* OF ADVERTISING

Convergence is simply a new application for brilliant creative. Come up with the mind-boggling, unbelievably brilliant, beyond-our-wildest-dreams creative. Now, let's challenge our marketing and creative team to turn these brilliant works of art, these masterpieces worthy of a roped-off section in the Louvre, to maintain this crowning achievement while transforming it to serve the performance of a V3 to at least a V5.

My challenge to you is to design the ad or messaging at several velocities while remaining respectful of the brilliant creative. You will be amazed at the outcome. I've watched teams work through this and discover a new way to balance the creative message to deliver higher performance by building brand resonance and not mere awareness ads in hopes of building a brand.

By shifting the very same root creative, embracing the concept of increasing the velocity of the same ad, the creative and marketing team can have the best of both worlds—a brilliant ad that has real traction.

Brilliant Creative at Work

In the early 1990s, AT&T ran a campaign of television commercials to compete against MCI. Both firms were into an all-out media war, and it was fun to watch. The AT&T campaign that still resonates for me was—We Want You Back. It was extremely creative, loaded with momentum and action, with a driving call to action. They used a large toll-free number; this was before we used the Internet, pushing viewers to make the switch.

I'm sure the budgets for these spots were out of sight for both firms, but they were using real-time accountable advertising. Static budgets went to dynamic investments, sending their media buys into the stratosphere. They understood their spend and gain every day, every week of their lives. Like the retailer down the street or the web marketer that is measuring because they can, this dynamic type of creative was everything it needed to be and more. They were in a battle for market share, and they had the ultimate tool to do it, great creative built into TV ads of the day to build brand and demand with the same budget at the same time. The media gods were appeased, and the beat went on. It doesn't get any better. And now the spots are on YouTube if you want to take a look.

Don't Let Your Babies Grow up to Be Cowboys

This is the story of one very green, longhaired, freshly minted MBA, who learned valuable life lessons about saloons, prairie oysters, and the genius behind a certain collectables firm in Cheyenne, Wyoming. I left the tie-dyed, peacenik college town of Eugene, Oregon for my first job out of grad school, in a town that existed because General Jackson told his troops to build a town where the mountains end. There is an old saying that the snow does not fall in Cheyenne, it blows clear into Nebraska.

It was the early 1980s, and the local bar scene was dominated by the locals, or, to put it plainly, the cowboys. After my first week at the new job, I and one of my new friends from work decided to go into town for a drink.

Standing at the bar in the Cheyenne Club, a big guy who looked like he lived out on the range with the deer and the antelope walked up and informed me that he didn't like my shirt. "I don't like your shirt [long pause], boy." I told him I was sorry about that and turned away, intending to ignore him. But ignoring him was impossible because he yelled over to his friend, "Hey, Red. Looks like we got one of those hippies in here." And from across the room this cowboy with red boots swaggers over to back his friend. My friend suggests we get the hell out of there, quick-like, as Red informs me, "Yep. We don't like your kind here [long pause], boy." The long pause preceding the word "boy" had psychotic implications. In an effort to grasp one remaining thread of manly composure, I took one more sip of my full beer, then abandoned it in hopes of a longer life span. We heard nothing but laughter and the pounding of our hearts as we walked out of that saloon.

From that point on, we were sentenced to the Holiday Inn at the crossroads of Interstates 25 and 80, next to the truck stop. Remember Bill Murray singing "Feelings" on *Saturday Night Live*? It was just like that. And riding my motorcycle on that barren plain below the foothills, I also noticed the acre of bunkers, seriously fenced off from the rest of the world, where some 200 missile silos scattered up and down the front range. Nothing like living at what could be ground zero.

So there must have been a compelling reason to stay there, and there was—the job. I was a project manager at a collectibles firm, and it changed my world, especially the way I look at marketing problems. That position gave me a whole new set of pragmatic tools that I continue to use when I analyze situations and develop marketing action steps. Over the years, I've honed those skills, and it's helped me bring in a lot of money with minimal risk. It's about tools and processes. Ninety-seven percent of everything I've worked on, representing over 2,000 campaigns over the past 20 years, made lots of money for my clients.

The president of this firm had the gift of knowing what would sell. He taught me to listen to my own counsel, to go with my gut, as they say. He instilled a love of marketing and advertising at the edge, and work was exciting enough to keep me, for a while, in this odd little town in the middle of nowhere. Then there was the VP of marketing, who was once the senior brand manager for Tide at Proctor & Gamble. Until he came to Cheyenne, his entire career was about building brand, yet he was the guy who taught me that the results achieved by using brand advertising alone were questionable. This was true on many levels, most importantly its inability to measure real-time results.

I was asked to assist with the largest promotion this firm had ever conceived. It ran across all of America; in *Parade, Family Weekly*, vertical trade and consumer magazines of many varieties, house and rented lists . . . and far too many to remember. I witnessed their ability to gamble away the farm . . . with confidence. This firm put almost half of its worth on the table to launch a program. How could they do this? What math were they working with? What were they smoking? But they knew their business so well that it wasn't even a question of whether they were going to make their numbers, but how much fine-tuning and adjustment was required. They knew their targets. They understood the demographics and the range of emotion their customers felt. They had looked into the very heart and soul of their customer. They also understood the role of the influencers. Their knowledge even extended to the *blockers*, those who try to *stop* purchasers, individuals seldom studied by most businesses. They understood and regularly reviewed their actual response rates, leading to the expected value of the individual, in all media. All variables were tested and kept on file, and the library held the wisdom of the firm. That library was our brain trust.

Whenever I was writing a plan, Bob, the research guy on staff, could give me a best guess on my response curves and how they would look *X* weeks out. His data was dynamically updated and always changing, but it gave me highs and lows on similar items with numeric probabilities. We tracked everything with the pure intent of mitigating our risk, and our opportunity, in both the short and long term.

The same approach can work for you. I have been doing this most of my life. This type of regimen has brought great wealth to all my clients who use it. Here's an example of how we used the data. (I can't believe I actually remember this stuff!) It was the early 1980s, and I worked on a plan to spend $200,000 on a full-page gate-fold in *National Geographic*. United States' circulation at the time was 8.4 million, with worldwide coming in at just over 12 million. We had never advertised in *National Geographic*, but we'd advertised in *The Smithsonian*, *Architectural Digest*, and other similar magazines that had good crossover. Bob and I started poring through all the response data one afternoon. With a range from high to low of only three-tenths of 1 percent, I knew with 70 percent or better confidence that I would achieve sales at .02, or two-tenths of 1 percent because our data showed that we had achieved this level many times before with other products. I needed only a .0075 sales response to break even. I had the data to make a sound business decision and, better yet, sleep well knowing I would bring in well over $1 million in orders with that ad. And I was right. This stuff does set you free.

THE WORKSHEET: TRANSFORMING THE WAY YOU SEE MARKETING AND ADVERTISING

It was a cool spring day in Austin, Texas. I was presenting an all-day seminar on convergence marketing at Advanced Micro Devices (AMD), the primary competition of Intel. The morning was spent going over theory and pragmatic case studies on Novell, Sybase, 3M, and five divisions of Lucent. All 45 participants were interested and involved. We spent the afternoon working with my Revised Budget Allocation worksheet using brand-interaction advertising via all media at optimum velocities.

Breaking into teams of five, the attendees were tasked with recrafting their respective budgets for the following year using what they had learned that day. What was usually an hour and a half exercise, complete with team presentations, turned into an entire afternoon work session. At 3:00 I tried to wrap it up, but they wouldn't hear of it. They were on a roll, determined to get the most out of their optimized marketing and advertising allocations.

Each team worked hard and debated how far could they push the velocity. Two directors helped out. It was a bullpen, with business unit managers and product marketing folks alike wrestling with the concepts of the AMD brand. Was an increase in velocity always good, or was there a breaking point? Print should have its own standard, mail another, web another. All found their comfort zone.

The Brand-Interaction Worksheet

The worksheet has six parts, signified by columns (see Figure 8.1). The primary purpose is to take your initial budget and determine the mix of media vehicles, and budget to invest, to drive the optimum number of BIPs (Brand Interaction Points). Your goal is not just to get interaction. It is to build brand and demand at the same time using all the convergence marketing tools and concepts I have outlined. Once proven and perfected for your business, it holds the foundation for your new and optimized go-to-market strategies.

Figure 8.1 The Brand-Interaction Worksheet

Medium	Typical Interaction Rate	Cost per Interaction	Velocity	Budget per Medium	Interactions per Medium
Brand Print Ads	0.05% to 0.1%	$600	1 – 3		
Brand-Interaction Print Ads	0.3% to 0.75%	$50 – $125	4 – 6		
Inserts	0.05%	$100 – $125	6 – 7		
Direct Mail	.25 to 2.0%	$75 – $200	2 – 4		
Brand-Interaction Direct Mail	1% to 7%	$20 – $100	5 – 7		
DRTV spot (not cable)	n/a	$40	7		
National Brand TV	n/a	$1,000	1		
Radio	n/a	$70 – $250	3 – 7		
Email Marketing	3% to 5%	$60 – $80	4 – 6		
Banner Advertising: Click thru	0.03% to 0.05%	$50 – $70	5		
Tradeshows	n/a	$100 – $200	7 – 10		
Paid Search		$1 – $10	5		
Organic Search		$1 – $10	5		
TOTAL					

1. Benchmark Where You Are Today

Outline your Sales Assumptions:

- Need sales of : Units _____ Sales Revenue _____

- Percent of trials appointments become sales _____
- Open A and B interactions needed _____
- Initial Advertising Budget to deliver goals _____

Starting on the left are media for you to consider, with both offline and online in the mix. Be sure to save money for PR.

Next, outlined in column two, is the typical interaction rate you may receive. These numbers represent a range. Use them as a benchmark to consider. Out of column two, column three will often follow.

You will need to gather information from a few locations to uncover the interaction rates for your respective business. Your demand-generation media will be the easiest portion to fill out. Do the same for print and broadcasting. You will figure it as a function of circulation. Determine a figure for both search vehicles. Set a benchmark to judge later. Find an index that is a placeholder to start. Make your assumptions as you would for any spreadsheet.

It may be shocking to see in writing what you have spent and what you can attribute to each media. This is the very reason for the exercise. Few people want to measure brand-focused print and television advertising at a V1 to V3 level, but it's important to measure *all* the media in use.

Column four is the velocity level. Study the TaylorMade ads in Chapter 4. Remember this is an art *and* a science. Fill out your typical interaction rates as best you can with your information. You should have all three columns filled in with swags or better. The very act of trying to fill out this worksheet will have you and your team searching for better answers in the future.

With all of this in place, the first pass is to take your existing budgets and fill in column five, budget per medium. Column six is for the interactions per medium. Take your budget in column five and divide it by your medium cost per interaction from column three. This will give you total the interactions per media. Write them in. Then add them all up and you'll have the total BIP score based on your historical spend.

2. Revise Your Budget Allocation

Take one more blank form and consider how the increase in velocity will increase other areas, such as awareness, consideration, and interaction rate of the communication. Apply that thinking and fill in columns one and two. Figure 8.2 outlines the projected increase in touch points as the velocity increases.

Next, revise your spend based on a give and take between media. More BIPs are preferred, and you'll discover the optimum balance for your company. Please see preceding sales assumptions and craft yours from the VP of sales.

What Should You Expect?

The participants in the seminar ended up with a rate four times higher than the traditional approach. Eighty brand managers at a

Figure 8.2 Brand Impact as a Function of Velocity

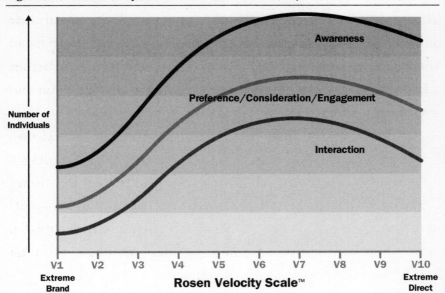

seminar at GM University reallocated a budget line $15,000,000 to stimulate one of their older car brands. Their result outperformed the previous 46,000 BIPs to a range of 130,000 to 160,000 BIPs, based on the group's strategy and tactics.

At one of the B-to-B seminars, the 70 participants went from 50,000 BIPs to over 250,000 BIPs. They were the most bullish of all groups, made up almost entirely of B-to-B direct marketers. A full-day seminar with John Deere Corporation increased their 50,000 BIPs to 200,000. The participants were managers from advertising, direct, product, and marketing. I've gone through this exercise with five different electric utility companies, and their results were similar to GM's, generating three times the BIPs of the traditional approach.

Each time I've presented the worksheet with a few hours allocated to go through it, the participants have increased their velocity. It has consistently increased by at least three times their current BIPs, across all media. Now it's your turn to see what magic you can perform to expand your budget. Gather your team and have fun.

9

THE BRAND-INTERACTION
ACCELERATOR™

The Brand-Interaction Accelerator is a graphic representation of all the phases of the convergence model. It is a tool that lets you see the dynamics of bringing brand and direct together. From creative that generates interaction to real-time accounting, it all works together to accelerate the old static budget into a dynamic, low-risk investment. Convergence is a living, breathing model that gives us constant feedback, informing us what works and what doesn't. It's the financial model used by Dell and others to kill their competition.

We begin with two concentric circles that connect in the middle (see Figure 9.1). The top circle represents "above the line," or what I call *brand-interaction building advertising*. The circle below represents "below the line," which includes direct, sales, and the

Figure 9.1 Brand-Interaction Accelerator™

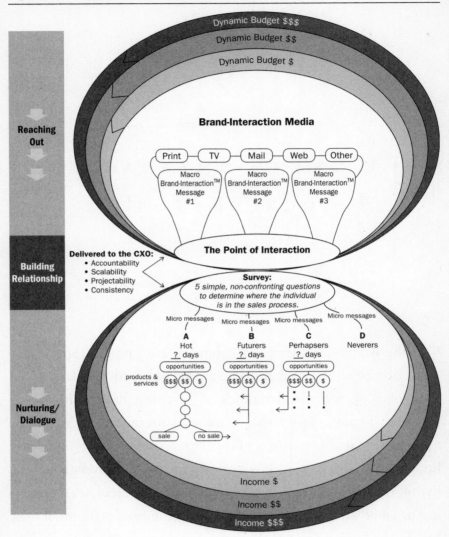

sales pipeline. The center area, where the two circles come together, is the point of interaction. Above and below the line influence each other with their information and creative. The essence of convergence is building brand and demand at the same time. We're going to leverage the budget to achieve dynamic and not static investment, which is represented by the outer rings of the circle. Knowing what is working in real time and investing in it to keep it going is the high coefficient that drives success. No one is held up waiting for budget to come in, and the C-suite is drooling over dashboard reports like they've never seen before. Convergence takes Integration to a whole new level. We can learn from the likes of Dell, Bose, Capital One, Geico, and the catalogers and web marketers, who have made a fortune using investment spending.

BRAND-INTERACTION MEDIA

Beginning with the upper circle, we have listed all the media that we can use to communicate our V3 to V8 message. This includes print, TV, mail, web, e-mail, search and others. Convergence relies on communications within the V3 to V8 to gain the interaction needed to move the individual forward. If we use creative with lower velocity, at a V1 or V2, we would not achieve the interaction we need to drive the model. For this model to work, you need to design communications that spark interaction. They will deliver the brand awareness of a V1 or V2, plus three to seven times the amount of BIPs, building brand resonance faster with less cash with far greater efficiency.

Next on the diagram, just beneath the row of media, we have macro messaging one, two, and three. This represents the two to three messages we'll use to go to market. For some, these are the primary messaging platforms that differentiate your product in the mind of the target. For example, TaylorMade Golf had two unique platforms. One was the legacy, associating the clubs with

Scotland and the roots of the game. The second was the technology and design of the clubs, giving you the extra 50 yards. Either one of these macro messages would appeal to the target, affording various layers of messaging at the same time.

The difference between using media in our new model, as opposed to the traditional model, is the ability to track the effectiveness of communications in real time. We can measure the different media and determine if one is pulling better than the others. If so, we can pull the weak performers and reinvest that money into the media that is pulling best.

The Point of Interaction

In the middle of these two circles is the point of interaction. It is the focal point of all of the creative media. Not only are we building awareness with the communications, but the creative executions have a high enough velocity to drive those who are ready to move forward into the sales process, *right now*. I think of this place as the meeting of two disciplines of thought. It is the place where we stop and reflect by measuring what our above-the-line communication has accomplished.

As outlined in the sales cycle and dialogue process, we're using appropriate offers to stimulate interaction. This proof of concept works best when we design the communication vehicle to push though awareness into engagement and then to interaction. This is the ultimate use of design and copy to build brand and demand across all vehicles at the same time.

We've driven three to seven times more individuals to interaction, building the company's greatest asset: interested individuals.

The best part is that we can talk to them in a one-to-one dialogue, and we've gotten here faster than ever before. The cost to build brand resonance has plummeted. In effect, the budget has increased because we have more left over, which we can use to repeat our process and drive sales.

Survey

We are going to ask our interested individuals, with great empathy and sensitivity, a few probing questions. We need to know where they are in the sales cycle, so that our next communication with them will pull them in further. We don't want to lose them by being too aggressive or too passive. We're only asking a few questions; I recommend no more than five.

Another way to find out where they are in the sales cycle is using another vehicle, like a microsite. We need to get them involved, and the web is a wonderful tool for personalization and interactivity. Seeing what they are responding to will provide us with the information we need to determine what to put in front of them next.

Nurturing the Interactions

From survey, we move further down the model, into the lower circle, or below the line. This is where we review the micro messages, or the information we've gathered on them in our database. We have coded most everything, so we know how they have come onto the record. We know what message stimulated them to get involved and their responses to the questions. We may not have every detail from each individual, but we have enough to determine the strategy and tactics to move them forward.

Classifying Leads for the Investment Spend

The center of the lower circle shows the categories, from A to D, where we determine the right classification for each individual. Based upon the information they've provided, we can determine whether the individual is an A, B, C, or D lead.

An A lead is hot. They're the furthest along in the sales cycle and represent, on average, between 7 percent to 15 percent of respondents. Their answers revealed buying signals, usually based on time or value.

I refer to B leads as *futurers*, or A leads in waiting. Representing some 35 percent to 50 percent of the respondents, we usually find that at least 10 percent of this group are A leads in hiding. We'll send the As to sales. The Bs have shown interest by taking us up on whatever offer we've put in front of them.

The next group, the Cs, are about 30 percent of the respondents. I call them the *perhapsers*. They might buy, someday, unlike our As who are ready now and our Bs who will buy in the future. However, we want to nurture them at some budget level.

The final category, representing about 20 percent, are the D leads. I call them *nevers*. These folks responded by not answering your questions at all or answering them falsely. They give bad numbers and e-mail address. They might be students who just wanted the free offer. But no matter who they are, it's clear they have no interest in buying.

Dynamic Investment

Around the two circles representing above-the-line and below-the-line advertising, the model shows the budgets growth based on real-time success. We go from dynamic budget one on the inner ring represented by one $, and increase as we expand to two $$ and then three $$$. These outer rings represent the continuous growth of investment spending on marketing, sales, and advertising. It's a constant flow of funds based on acquiring and selling new and existing customers in a dynamic function.

The Infinity Loop

This graphic representation of convergence shows all of the workings above and below the line and wraps it with an infinity loop of dynamic investment. By this I mean that the budget continues to expand as our costs per acquired interaction shrinks. We have more money to invest in future communications as we loop around the lower circle several times, building financial momentum, and carrying those funds into the upper loop, to spend on above-the-line communications. The loop also symbolizes the influential relationship between the two circles. Communications above the line are crafted using information from below the line to drive interaction to the lower circle. At the same time, the activities below the line are influenced by the actions and communications above the line to categorize and nurture the leads. The old model kept the circles separate, but convergence uses this influential relationship to build brand resonance. The endless loop is unstoppable and shows just how convergence can grow the business with precision and low risk.

Convergence and the C-Suite

Last, but certainly not least, is the crucial relationship with the C-suite and how they feed the marketing and advertising engine.

Historically, they've had to fuel it as a line item on their cost sheet, pumping cash from other revenues to feed the monster. They want you to deliver accountability, scalability, projectability, and consistency. Now you can.

WHAT HAPPENS WHEN WE PUT IT ALL TOGETHER

You understand convergence and are armed with the tools and the Velocity Scale, so what's next? Here's a scenario. Let's create two big messaging platforms, with great creative at a V4 on the Velocity Scale. It's a little different than the usual V1 advertisements, but it has great creative, and it's engaging. Now you have people responding in record numbers. It's exciting to see the traction with this new campaign. Your print vehicle is on fire, delivering four times the usually number of people to the microsite alone. There's a buzz throughout marketing and advertising as you pass in the halls. Every one seems to be smiling. A few days later, the CFO pops his head in to see what's going on. The buzz increases as the rumors kick in. Your above-the-line communication is working really well. Early indicators predict a home run.

Everything is moving to the point of interaction. Both messaging platforms are tracking well with one outpulling the other by almost two to one. Most individuals are filling out your short survey. The white paper is working to no end. All of a sudden, holy cow, the A leads are coming in at 12 percent, Bs are at 45 percent, and it is a very good day. Two weeks later, the sales team makes their first sale. You check the database and see that the lead came in from your print vehicle.

Another week passes, and the sales team is ecstatic. The presentations from print that hit first are working better than anyone anticipated. You're all watching for the e-mails and mail to start hitting. It's amazing. The B lead nurturing system is up and running, and the first pass reveals 7 percent were A leads in hiding. You send them to the sales team. The C leads were sent a simple e-mail and the Ds a nice thank you note for responding. Everything is working. The bottom circle is spinning, representing all of the forces at work to nurture and bring home the sales. The pipeline is full, yet we know it can handle more.

Three weeks pass, and the numbers are indisputable. Print is coming in at $125 per BIP, a much lower cost than the usual $300 to $600 per BIP. Mail is at $40, and e-mail is really inexpensive, coming in at only $5 per BIP, but you're out of names. Television is even down, at around $40 per BIP. It is clear that one of two platforms is outperforming the other, so you decide to shift all media to the stronger platform.

Leads continue to pour in via all media. The funnel is full. The pipeline is full. The company is loving it and can handle more. The numbers from both the top and the bottom of the model are clear. The cost per sale is the lowest you have ever seen. The sales team proclaims a day in your honor.

Your first dynamic budget is spent, but you know how to get more. You have the technology, the sales, and financial proforma in real-time, so you walk into the CFO's office and lay out a statistically sound business case. You can, for the first time in your career, speak the same language. You know what you've spent and your return to gross interaction. You know what your A and B leads cost. You know your closing ratio on A leads, and you can estimate what the B leads are worth over time. It is scaleable with 95 percent confidence. All you have to do is outline why the company should invest more in this program, which carries extremely low business risk. After a few meetings the C-suite is on board, demanding you seize the day.

Dynamic investment budget number two rolls out and feeds the advertising machine. It runs more efficiently than the first time, and returns follow suit. Everyone is watching. The results hold. Interactions come in, surveyed and classified. The As go to the sales, and the Bs are set up for nurturing.

Around and around the bottom wheel goes. Just when you're getting ready to present another full business case to the CFO for more funds, he shows up at your office and says, "Listen, I would like you get as many customers as we can this quarter at two hundred dollars per customer. If you can do this, you can have access to a line I'll set up for you. I want to try something new. Instead of basing it on last years' sales, it's going to be based on a function of what we can afford to spend to get as many new customers in the door as possible. This is directly from the CEO." Then he asks you if you'd like to become a member of his club. He'd be happy to sponsor you.

You are actualizing dynamic investment budget number three. The infinity loop is unstoppable, going around and around the top, generating interactions, then flowing them into bottom, going around and around and then back to the top. The infinity loop, the ultimate branding and sales machine, keeps on going. It's a great day to make money.

You have experienced the convergence marketing model, and you are unstoppable.

III

PERFORMANCE AND BALANCE

10

ZEN AND THE ART OF . . .
THE MOTORCYCLE STORY

When I was very young, fearless, and in love with going fast, I raced motorcycles. Back then I got my kicks out of going 130 miles per hour down the back stretch of the raceway in Loudon, New Hampshire. Occasionally, I'd end up piled into a corner with 20 other bikes, which was not so much fun.

Getting ready for a race was no small task, and one day in particular I was having a problem getting my bike as perfect as I needed it to be. In the process of fine-tuning every detail to achieve maximum speed with safety and everything in perfect order, I had somehow missed the concept of balance. Missing this minute detail caused me to go into a speed wobble. Imagine flying down a racetrack at incredible speed when all of a sudden, at about 115 miles per hour, the bike starts vibrating and shaking into an impossible-to-control wobble that nearly threw me off the track. It was, to say the least, scary. I did everything I could to make every part of my bike perform at its best, but I learned later that day that my back and front tire were not perfectly balanced. Had I balanced my tires individually and then together, I would have been able to reach my optimum performance.

We Can Fly

This is the perfect analogy for the struggles we face in our silo culture of marketing and advertising. We can move at a low speed, and we don't experience any real problems. But if we rev things up to a higher performance level, we experience all sorts of blow outs stemming from the wobble of imbalance. The only way to recover is to return to a lower speed in order to protect the investment, just like I had to lower my speed to get out of the wobble, and then slow down even more to keep from damaging my bike, which was the investment of my boss at the motorcycle shop. Plus, that wobble took one heck of a toll on my body.

Finding balance within my communications has been my life's work. I think the same holds true for all of us in marketing and advertising, and I'm convinced that the only way to find that perfect balance to experience optimum performance is through convergence. We share the same goals, we find our common language, we learn from each other and appreciate the brilliance we all bring to our common table, and that is how we fine-tune our organizations. We can deliver so much more, leveraging our resources to increase profit beyond our wildest dreams. In perfect balance, we can fly.

11

A FEW MORE CASE STUDIES

The proof is in the pudding—or, should I say, in the ice cream. Each of the following case studies used convergence tools to create unprecedented results and profits. I attacked different problems in different industries and markets and was usually successful beyond the clients' wildest dreams. All of the tools and tactics I've provided are validated in these case studies, which I hope will inspire you to plunge in head first and start making your own profit—or pudding, as it were.

TANGO

Pervasive Software in Austin wanted to introduce both webmasters and novice web developers to its new web development tool, Tango 2000 Development Studio. Because few people in the target audience had ever heard of the company, let alone the product, my challenge was to overcome a number of objections. I needed to get beyond what might seem to be another *me-too* product and persuade them to invest in the learning curve of this new product. In addition, Pervasive was also looking to gain market share from its biggest competitor, Cold Fusion. We had one million potential users to target with one integrated media campaign.

Rather than following the look and tone of most high-tech ads of the day, which looked like a boring data sheet, we went the other way. We created an integrated multimedia campaign for Tango 2000 that used nontech graphics and copy that stimulated interaction with the target audience. However, the key to our success was knowing our target. We started out knowing that the target was made up almost entirely of young men. Initially, the client suggested that the offer should be a sweepstakes for a free one-year lease on a Porsche Boxster. My team thought a trip for two to Buenos Aires, the home of the tango dance, would be cool. But our focus groups gave both ideas a unanimous thumbs-down.

So we needed more research to see who this target really was. For this exercise, I highly recommend gathering your team in a closed room with a whiteboard. Start by laying out what you know about the target. Ask questions like, what do they wear, what kind of car do they drive, do they go out to theaters or bars? Do they drink beer or wine, what kind? Do they have time on their hands? Do they have hobbies? Do they like to hike or play tennis? Are they loaded with cash and ready to buy, or are they influencers? What's inside their refrigerator? What's on their walls? Do they rent or own a home? Do they surround themselves with white walls or do they prefer color? Don't forget to add the business issues that surround the selling environment into the mix. I like to put percentages of confidence next to each variable so that I can see how much I know for sure, especially on variables that are critical. If you see that you don't have a good handle on scoping out these individuals, you need to invest in more research.

For the Tango campaign, we used a combination of survey questions and focus groups, and both were invaluable in shaping our messaging as well as the ask and offer platforms. Here's what we found out. Our target was a young male, aged 22 to 28, who ate a lot of pizza, didn't go out much except to movies, spent an ungodly number of hours at his computer, and was extremely competitive with software such as games, but not at all athletic. He drove a really great car but had no social life. He didn't date, not so much from choice, but from lack of social interaction.

This information helped us create a program that spoke directly to him. We appealed to his desires as well as his competitive nature. We got his attention with the type of woman he would like to date, young, attractive, and little on the sultry side, and she invited him to Tango. We pulled them in even further with the promise of fast software, which they could try out in a competition for a really cool home workstation. It was everything they wanted, and we knew it. Taking the step to really know the individual was the foundation that made this campaign one of the biggest successes of my career (See Figure 11.1).

Rather than following conventional high-tech advertising that looked like a data sheet, we created a series of ads that exploded from the pages of publications with non-high-tech

Figure 11.1   Tango Print Ad #1, Don't Be a Web-Flower, V6

visual energy. We capitalized on the obvious connection to Latin dancing with photos of a couple dancing for the ads and a video for the microsite. The print ad shown here was a V6, and it drove our target to the microsite to register for the sweepstakes and get the free software. The headline challenged our guy to get in step and not be a "web-flower."

The second ad (Figure 11.2) was a V3, and it encouraged more interaction by offering free training in addition to the free software. The core of the offer was the free Tango 2000 Studio software, and to get it, all they had to do was register. Of course, the back-end was an eventual upgrade to the $3,500 application server. Previous campaigns had told us this audience had access to high bandwidth connections, but even we were surprised that a full 60 percent of respondents downloaded the software instead of waiting for the CD fulfillment.

The fulfillment package shown in Figure 11.3 was a V4. The Tango 2000 program balanced the four variables and used all media relative to the target. The Tango campaign was empathetic to their desires. It found them where they hung out. Mail vehicles went to their offices; ads were placed in technology magazines they read.

A V1 brand awareness commercial (see Figure 11.4) went on the screens of the Austin cinemas that they frequented. Each communications led them to a video on a microsite that engaged them with the product. (See Figures 11.5 and 11.6)

The results were amazing. With an initial budget of about one-half million dollars, we generated 40,000 online registrations over a 120-day period, with 15,000 of those registrations coming in the first 30 days. We shortened the response cycle

Figure 11.2 Print Ad #2, Reignite Your Passion for the Web, V3

Figure 11.3   Tango Fulfillment Package, V4

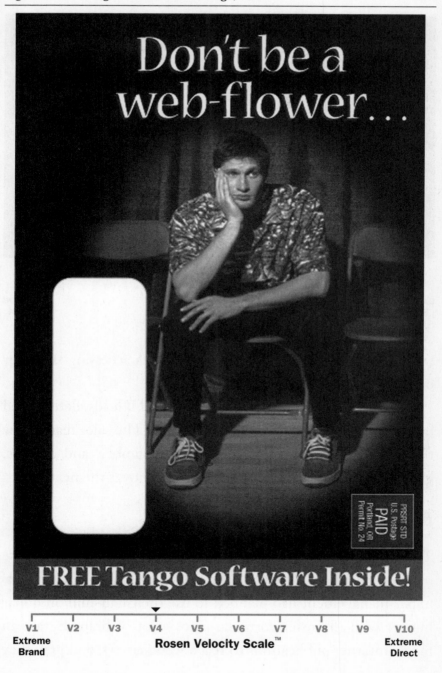

Figure 11.4   Tango Theatre Ad, V1

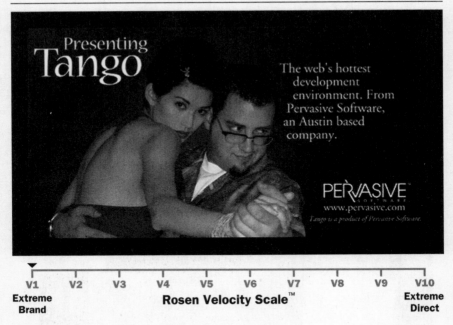

with approximately 60 percent of prospects accessing the offer on the web for faster fulfillment.

Over 60 percent of our guys were A and B leads, determined by their answers to five probing questions. The sales team knew their classification, their e-mail, phone number, and address, given with permission to continue dialogue over the next year.

Lessons Learned from Tango

There were a number of lessons learned from this campaign, the main one being that convergence works really well. Our clients' upper management had planned to use their half-million dollar budget with the usual formula, place a lot of branding ads in major Internet publications to reach web masters, and pray they

Figure 11.5 Tango Microsite, V5

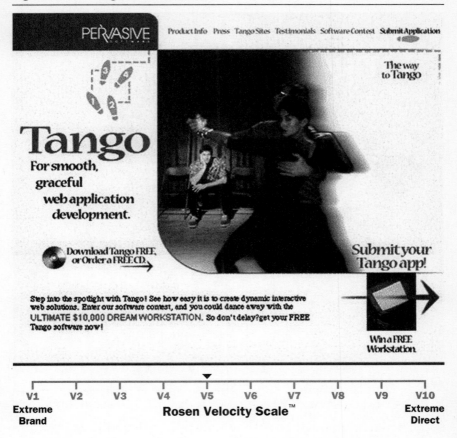

would come running to buy the new software. Unrealistic, to say the least. Simply launching a new product into that market space, with such existing clutter, would have been suicidal.

Could we have accomplished what we did if we had followed the traditional model? Not on your life. The technology space was overcrowded and the noise was overwhelming. No matter how brilliant the creative or on-target the message, they didn't have the funds to drive the frequency it would have needed to stand out. But our strategic plan using the convergence methodology

Figure 11.6   Tango Web Video Still, V5

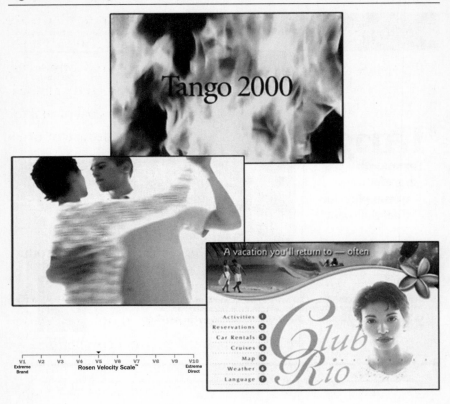

was successful beyond the clients' expectations. Frankly, the very process, as a tool to generate brand resonance while reducing risk and achieving the sales goal, has worked 97 percent of the time throughout my career.

An Important Variable Too Often Overlooked: How Does the Client Make Money?

Marketing and advertising must know how the client makes money. We were hired to create ads that would position and sell

Tango against the number one player, Cold Fusion. In order to create success for my client, I had to understand how they make money. Was it by selling the software programs at $500 a pop, or selling servers at several thousand dollars a pop? Considering they had a better profit margin on the servers, I used that knowledge to craft a campaign that would achieve their goal of making lots of money. That's right; we gave away the software in order to sell servers.

Combining this information with our new understanding of the prospect, the young webmaster, we wanted to create something more engaging for him or her than just buying software. We discovered that these webmasters would jump at the challenge to use our software to compete for something they really wanted. And what they really wanted was a powerful home workstation. We could engage them by giving them the software and challenging them to develop a sample site in a competition for the big prize—a powerful home workstation.

It worked. We got them involved. We moved them to interaction and brand resonance in record time and leveraged a small budget because we knew who "they" were.

The Key Variable: The Rosen Velocity Scale This Tango ad is hard-hitting, emotional, and engages the reader through strong headlines and call to action, while complimenting the brand. It's a V6 on The Rosen Velocity Scale. Those of you from the direct marketing side are probably questioning the use of reversed-out copy. I initially had the same reaction. But my creative director needed the dark background to set the romantic mood and stimulate the interaction. We had a great call to action, an engaging sweepstakes, and were right on the money in our tone and execution to get our target to move forward in the sales process. We had art and copy working together in a most responsive and brand-enhancing manner. Wow, strong copy, strong art, and strong call to action to drive engagement, leading to interaction and nurture of the sale. It all worked!

FRONTERA: DOGS AND ICE CREAM

Frontera was already a successful enterprise application service provider (ASP) providing web-based e-business solutions. At the same time, they realized they needed to boost their brand awareness in order to stand out in an aggressive and competitive market. They changed their focus from Internet services to application services in 2001, hoping to take advantage of an emerging market for outsourced e-business solutions. However, stiff competition from established ASP leaders made things rough for the company. Analyst reports favored outsourcing for lowering costs and relieving the headaches brought on by trying to manage software and servers. Yet Frontera was getting drowned out by the noise of their competition. At the same time, they were dealing with internal repercussions of corporate spending cutbacks.

The good news was that they had the right stuff to take on the competition. They offered easy, affordable solutions to the troublesome cost and hassle of managing technology in-house. Backed by strong partners like BEA and e-piphany, Frontera provided expert technical service, great customer care and affordable, scalable software. Early customers included Pioneer Electronics and

Conseco, two large, well-respected firms that reported high satisfaction with Frontera's service and value. So I had to figure out how we could increase their presence on the radar screen.

Clearly, we needed to build brand awareness for the company in the general marketplace and generate qualified leads for its sales team. My team and I created a campaign that utilized print advertising, e-mail, and direct mail, incenting the customer to visit a microsite. The microsite explained highlights and benefits of Frontera's service offerings and collected data from prospects. We wanted to lift Frontera's profile while encouraging response and setting the tone for upcoming sales calls.

Frontera's campaign opened with a V3 e-mail that led to a microsite that served both IT and C-level prospects. The nontopical offer was the magical coupon for free Häagen-Dazs ice cream, which they could enjoy while reading the topical offer of a white paper on the benefits of e-business outsourcing. All they had to do was answer a few questions to get the goods. Others would receive a personalized 9" × 12" mail vehicle and letter that showed how Frontera's solutions benefited Pioneer Electronics. It was sent in two waves to pace response. Mailing lists, intended for C-level and IT executives, were rented from *Red Herring Magazine* and *Dun & Bradstreet*. These lists provided current, accurate names and titles for companies that fit our target profile. Frontera also provided a select list of qualified names.

In addition to all of this, we placed V6 full-page print ads in the *L.A. Business Journal* to build awareness and interaction in a city that was a major concentration for Frontera sales. The ads were placed during the same month that mailers were distributed. See figures 11.7 and 11.8.

Figure 11.7   Frontera Brand-Interaction Print Ad, V6

Figure 11.8   Frontera Brand-Interaction Microsite, V6

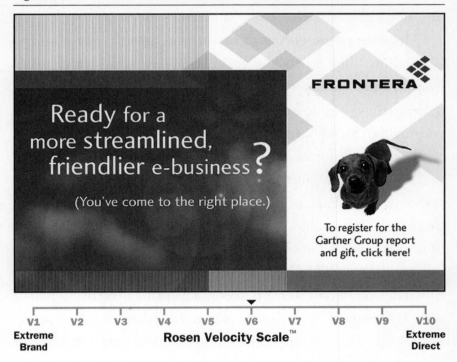

Frontera had some major objections to overcome. Companies need fast, affordable, durable, and reliable technology for their e-business solutions. They assume the big providers have the staying power they need. They can't afford for their customers to have bad experiences because they might get frustrated and never return. Plus, they assume the process of finding new providers will be painful, hassle-prone, and costly.

The message platform spoke directly to those fearful objections—be friendly and open while everyone else is uptight. Be the small, approachable company prospects can relate to instead of a monolithic corporation. Use symbols, messages, and service descriptions that are empathetic. Make e-business an opportunity, not a problem. Rest easy—and eat some ice cream.

The offers were perfect. I mean, who doesn't love Häagen-Dazs? Plus, they received a reliable, independent white paper from Garner Group that explained the costs and benefits of outsourcing e-business solutions. Frontera was clearly a company you could trust, who would take care of you, who wanted to make sure you were informed, and was your friend in the business.

The campaign's initial e-mail wave generated a .003 percent response rate. Part of this strong result was attributed to a carefully written subject line for the CXO audience. Two waves of printed mail vehicles, a total of 60,000, delivered a 6 percent interaction rate. This outperformed their previous V3 mail, which delivered only .0025 percent. The print advertising pulled over .005 percent to gross circulation, far exceeding their previous V1 ads. Overall, the entire campaign delivered *5 to 10 times better than any of their previous campaigns.*

Overall, the combination of positioning Frontera as the *rest easy* option, messages tailored for the right audience, our multi-touch delivery sequence, and flexible response mode delivered response rates that exceeded goals by well over 50 percent across the board. Best of all, Frontera sales teams were able to achieve high conversion-to-sale rates because of the quality of the leads.

12

THE LAST WORD

A few years ago, I heard Clayton M. Christensen, Harvard professor and leading authority of innovation management and disruptive innovation, give a presentation at a business conference in San Francisco. He asked us to consider "what a product is hired to do." He used the example of a McDonald's milkshake, which had unusually high sales during the morning rush hour in areas where drivers had long commutes. Most of us would assume that the line around the drive-thru window would be for the coffee hit, not the milkshake. So why the preference for a milkshake? Most of us assumed, referring back to his question, that the milkshake had been hired to quench a craving or fulfill a breakfast need for the consumer. But we were wrong. They discovered that commuters preferred the milkshake because it took a long time to drink. The thick liquid took a slow journey through the straw, giving them something to do during the long drive to work. It was their companion. Christensen concluded that the job the milkshake was hired to do was to keep the driver occupied during the long commute. The milkshake actually had a higher purpose.

It's an important question to consider as we hock our products and services to the world. But think about it in a personal way. What job have we been hired to do? The assumptions for marketing, advertising, and sales are pretty broad. How do we define our true role and actualize our higher purpose, like the milkshake?

The assumption of our separate roles in the established silos, locked in place by years of the refrain "this is the way we've always done it" has forced us into isolation. But in reality, we all share the same job. That's right. All of us in advertising, marketing, and sales have the same job: to make money for the client. It's no different than the NASA story, and acknowledging that we are all in this together will make the cultural shift a lot easier as we move toward convergence.

Change will be even easier if the folks at the top understand and support it. They will jump onboard if you present convergence as a way to increase profits across all areas of the business. They might even design a new organization chart that brings the silos together. If they can design bonuses and rewards for the combined results of the team, well, you'll be cooking.

I've seen it happen. The CEO brings the VP of sales, the CMO, and the VP of brand into a conference room, and we present this methodology, along with the Velocity Scale, and how it all works together. Once they try it and like it, there's no going back. It makes too much sense to ignore the possibilities,

Figure 12.1   Cost per Sales Drops as Velocity Increases

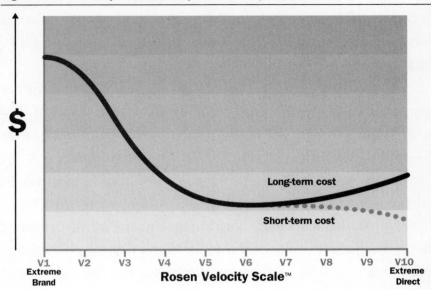

and the process of change is really not that overwhelming. You can begin with the work you do at whatever level you're at. But it's definitely easier when the C-level folks buy in.

The financial benefits are huge, and laid out simply in Figures 12.1, 12.2, 12.3, and 12.4, which show the leverage convergence will deliver.

SEEING THE RESULTS

The graph in Figure 12.1 shows how the cost per sale drops as the velocity increases. I call it the death curve. It's very hard to get any traction at a velocity of V1 to V3, and the cost of acquisition is, without fail, out of sight. This is where 95 percent of all adverting in trade print and television lives. We tested this many times in various media when Wall Street approached Dell asking them to look more grown-up. We went down that road for a bit, but quickly returned to our roots. It was too expensive and, more important, didn't give reliable metrics.

We needed to drive a scalable machine, understanding what every dollar spent would cost us, and what it would return. We were building brand, one customer at a time. Communication at V4 would not work at V3 and below. It was that simple.

We knew that borrowing the money we needed to spend on advertising was both a short-term and a long-term investment. Growing wallet-share and, more important, market share against our static-budget competitors like IBM and Compaq Computer, gave Dell the edge. We were unstoppable. You, too, can adopt these new-found creative relationships using velocity as one more major factor in your tool box of new absolutes.

Figure 12.2　Brand Impact as a Function of Velocity

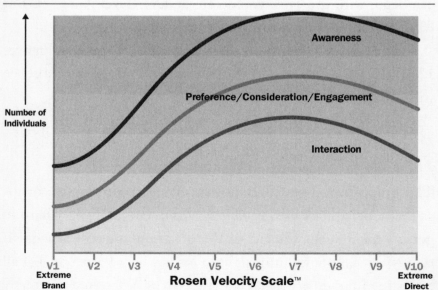

Taking this one step further, Figure 12.2 is the inverse of Figure 12.1. Think of this as a dashboard for all of management. As you increase velocity, you increase brand impact and awareness. Your preference and interaction scores will also increase.

A print ad at a velocity of V4 to V7 delivers three to seven times the interactions over an ad designed at a velocity of V1 to V3 using similar creative. These are all mutually inclusive events. Building awareness and preference scores while building brand at the same time, well . . . you now have the secret sauce to deliver untold leverage. Figure 12.2 has earned over 80 percent confidence from industry leaders in both brand and direct disciplines with both online and offline media. Refinement is our next step to even better profits.

Another valid reason for adopting convergence marketing is the effect it has on new product introductions. We surveyed over 100 executives at director-level or above, from both brand and direct disciplines, to achieve confidence with Figures 12.3 and 12.4

Figure 12.3 shows three lines, representing a communication at V1, V2, and V3.

Notice that the break-even point occurs very late when using low velocity communication.

Figure 12.4 shows the results when you increase the velocity. The curves start out slow with pure awareness building. Increasing the velocity to stimulate more customers to dialogue with you sooner allows you to build brand resonance faster with less money. All this ads up to the curves taking you past break-even faster and at a steeper slope. Very exciting!

Figure 12.3 Break-even Occurs Later with a Lower Velocity

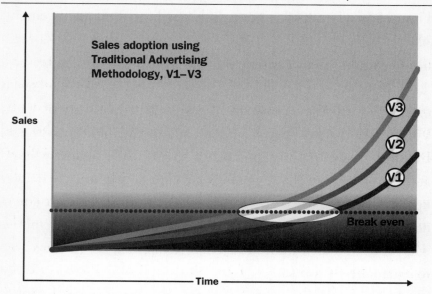

Figure 12.4 Raising the Velocity Brings Profit Much Sooner

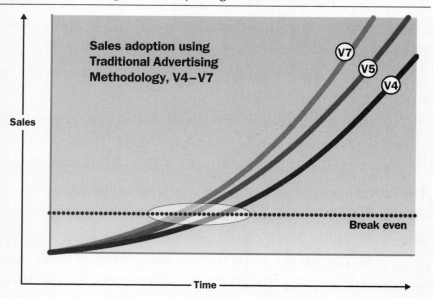

RUNNING TO THE NEXT MEDIA

Of course, the web has changed everything. It has forced both disciplines to converge faster than anytime in history. 1.0 web was exciting, 2.0 is just getting going. There are many paths and many roadblocks yet to come. Some will make fortunes, while others will be no more than hype, with only the few who sold the supplies making money. Working alongside this new frontier are the old media; print, mail, TV, and radio. Some are still working well—others, not so much. Mail still works well, giving us a tactile medium that is refreshing in our electronic world. TV is in need of help, due, no doubt, to the onslaught of channels in American homes. Time shifting, video clips, and pod delivery will be the new venue for *the spot* moving forward. Radio is still strong, and newspapers, though hovering, are still the leading vehicle for retail.

The report on print is mixed. According to the numbers, print is losing out fast to the web. Clients and agencies alike are not generating the scores needed to sustain the media. Print, the almighty brand vehicle of the past century, is losing its place as the ultimate brand instrument. But convergence has the means to turn it around. Convergence will redefine print and return it to its status as the powerhouse it was in the past. Who doesn't appreciate a wonderful ad in a beautiful magazine or publication? All media buyers agree; there is something about print that works.

I invite you to reconsider print. Experience it in a new way. Take brilliant creative and challenge your teams to create ads at the velocity of V4 through V7. Use strong headlines, good copy, and a reason for the individual to interact. It will deliver all I have promised. Face it; we all love print—we just want a new way of thinking about it. It needs a facelift, a change of architecture. Convergence marketing, along with the use of the Velocity Scale and the power of the Brand-Interaction Accelerator, are all tools worth exploring. The leverage can make you unstoppable.

Migrating from offline to online media, spending is off the charts. You don't want to bring the myopic silos of the past into the new world of all media working together. So let's pose our earlier question to our communications. What job have advertisers and marketers been hired to do? What job have we crafted it for? Is it the first, second, or fifth step in the sales process? Applying the methods and tools of convergence, how might you reshape your communications into all media to do their jobs with greater purpose and efficiency?

We live in a world that revolves around individuals. It's our job to help them celebrate with every product they buy. Convergence gives you the tools to help them decide to choose you, to communicate with you, to want what your brand has to offer. Your job is to create the right environment so they will want to give you access. In other words, you have to show them that you love them. Empathize with them, respect them, and regain their trust so they can trust the brand. It's the only path to achieve enduring brand loyalty.

There are a number of ways to get in on the dialogue. Join us at www.rgrosen.com find the level of interaction that works for you.

Converging brand and direct is easy, and you're already halfway there.

INDEX